HOUSEHOLD STRUCTURE IN THREE ENGLISH MARKET TOWNS, 1851-1871

DEREK CONSTABLE

geographical papers

Reading Geographical Papers
Department of Geography
University of Reading
Whiteknights Reading England
RG6 2AB

Published May 1977

ISBN   0 7049 0465 9

ISSN   0305 5914

Editors

Michael Batty Richard Foster Laurie Pickup Brian Preston

Printed by George Over Ltd., London and Rugby

CONTENTS

i

ABSTRACT

This research report presents the results of a 10% sample of dwelling-houses in the towns of Horsham, Sussex, and Salisbury and Swindon, Wiltshire, for the years 1851, 1861 and 1871. The data are contained in the Census Enumeration Books for each of those years, and are available in the Census Room of the Public Record Office in Portugal Street, London. The method of collecting, storing and processing the data is described and the problems of interpretation are discussed in detail. Some tentative conclusions are drawn from the data, but its presentation in table form in the Appendix enables social and economic historians, town planners, estate managers and others interested in nineteenth-century towns and town growth, the opportunity to study, test their own hypotheses and draw their own conclusions.

ACKNOWLEDGEMENTS

My thanks go to those in the Department of Geography, University of Reading: to Professor Peter Hall and Mike Batty for their assistance in choosing the towns for this study, and especially to Brian Preston and Mark Ebery for their advice on methods of data collection and analysis. I also wish to thank the University of London Computer Centre for programming assistance and for providing computer time for the data analysis, and especially the South Bank Polytechnic Faculty of Construction Technology and Design for their continual encouragement and provision of a research time allowance. In particular the author would like to thank the proprietors of Punch Magazine for permission to reproduce their cartoons. Appreciation is also extended to Brian Rogers for producing the cover and Jennifer Preston for typing the manuscript.

Derek Constable is currently a staff member in the School of Surveying, Thames Polytechnic, and is studying for a higher degree in the Department of Geography, University of Reading.

THE CENSUS.

Head of the Family (filling up the paper). "WELL, MISS PRIMROSE, AS A VISITOR, I MUST PUT YOUR AGE IN! WHAT SHALL WE SAY?"
Miss P. "OH, IT'S BEST TO BE STRAIGHTFORWARD. THE SAME AS DEAR FLORA. TWENTY LAST BIRTHDAY!"

1. AIMS OF THE RESEARCH

It is necessary to be quite specific in describing what this research report provides in order to prevent any mis-understandings and to provide a basis for other researchers who may use the results. The research was based on a 10% sample of the properties in each town. Each enumeration district book has the number of properties on the summary schedules at the beginning, and 10% of this figure, rounded up or down, provided the number of properties to be selected from that district. This method excluded all Institutions which have their occupants listed in the Enumeration Institution Schedules: the Work Houses, Lunatic Asylums and Infirmaries. In addition, those Institutions listed in the normal household enumeration books were excluded if they were selected by the sampling procedure and another property selected, so that all boarding schools, railway houses and common lodging houses were excluded.[1] The final result is, therefore, a sample of properties containing households having a family structure, with domestics and lodgers included where they occur. These results cannot be directly compared with the results of other research in this field, but similarly much of this work cannot be directly compared together.[2] Where possible, use was made of previously adopted coding methods to provide a basis for comparison, but complete standardisation was impossible.[3]

The results of the research described here are subsequently to be used for studies of the growth process of towns in terms of their buildings and, therefore, concentrates on household character rather than kinship patterns. This means that details of mothers-in-law, nephews, nieces and other relations and visitors are only superficial, whereas lodgers, shared households and multiple occupation of properties are important and are thus investigated in detail.

How useful are the research results produced in the tables? At the broad level they provide an interesting look at nineteenth-century society in three towns in the south of England; at the detailed level they provide significant information about family size, children living at home, age, occupation, and county of origin. However, for many minor matters there is an inadequate sample for much confidence to be placed in the results. The physical character of the towns studied, their size and history obviously affect their populations so that direct comparisons between communities is probably a worthless exercise, but the use of the results to draw conclusions which may be applicable to other similar towns may be worthwhile.

2. INTRODUCTION

As part of a study of town growth, the author had to collect time-series data and the most immediate source of relatively accurate small-scale data is the books of original returns for the National Censuses of 1851, 1861 and 1871. (Later books from 1881 onwards are protected from public scrutiny by the 'hundred year rule', and although the 1841 returns are available they are not as detailed as the later returns). The returns for these

1

censuses provide a list of the persons in each household, their names, sex, age, relationship to the head of the household, occupation, and parish and county of origin. The details for the individual households were collected by a process of dividing the country up into Registrars Districts, Sub-Districts and, the smallest area, the Enumeration District, and the returning officer of each Enumeration District delivering a form to be completed by the head of each household, or by the Enumerator if the head of the household could not complete the form himself. The Enumerators then took the individual household forms and copied out the details of each household in their areas, usually consisting of between 200 and 400 properties, into the books which are now held by the Public Record Office.[4] To identify the Enumeration District which covers any property or part of a town the Public Record Office provides indexes of towns and villages from which the relevant Enumeration District number or numbers can be found. By searching through the Enumeration Books the properties can be located by their address, or the description of the Enumeration District boundary at the front of each book, can be used to find the books covering the area of investigation. (This process may be quite complicated as most country properties have no addresses, addresses are occasionally missing even in urban areas, and sometimes the description of the area covered by the Enumeration District is missing from the front of the books). It is most unfortunate that the Public Record Office has only an incomplete set of maps for one of the census years showing Registration District boundaries and a few Enumeration District boundaries, because accurate cross-referencing between books of maps and Enumeration Books would be very useful. The usual method is to search all the Enumeration descriptions until the area of one's interest has been found and all the Enumeration Districts covering the area have been identified. Copies of medium scale (six inches to the mile) Ordnance Survey Maps are most useful, and copies of the early editions are available from the British Museum Map Room, although there is a delay for photocopying.

The Public Record Office provides the researcher with a microfilm of the Enumeration Books for use on a microfilm reader, but although this may safeguard original documents, the microfilm is an inadequate representation of the original. The records were written in ink, but many counts, alterations, ticks and other marks have been added, usually in pencil, and all this, when photographed in black and white, often obscures much of the information, especially in the 'ages' column. Some of the microfilms are photographed so that two small frames occupy the same space usually taken by one normal frame, and these small frames cannot be enlarged by the microfilm reader to interpret unclear words or numbers. The original records are much clearer, but are not easily available.

There has been surprisingly little quantitative research carried out using this census material. The pioneering work generally reported in Wrigley[5] and some other studies carried on since,[6] have hardly sampled this very rich source of data. One of the problems this raises is the general accuracy of the census returns, for until a larger amount of this data has been studied, only relatively superficial conclusions regarding its accuracy can be made, and these conclusions may only be valid for the area studied. Some of the likely inaccuracies in the census records are considered later, but it is certain that there were major differences in the skills of the Enumerators and substantial variations in the treatment of some matters by Enumerators in two or more adjacent districts. Any researcher is, therefore, strongly recommended to study not only the Enumeration Districts of particular interest to him, but also a few more from the immediate surroundings to see if any biases or methods peculiar to some Enumerators can be found. Obviously the identification of peculiarities in treatment may not be corrected; all that may be possible is a warning of their existence and the distortion likely to result.[7]

3. DATA COLLECTION, STORAGE AND ANALYSIS

The methods of collecting the data from the Enumerator's books were governed by the proposed use of the Statistical Package for the Social Sciences (SPSS) for its storage and subsequent analysis.[8] The SPSS is a specially designed computer package of statistical routines for social science data and is easily understood and used by people with little skill in computer programming. This package was recommended, by other workers in the field, as being the most suitable, was also being used by the Hampshire County Council for the storage and manipulation of town planning statistics, and was available at the University College London Computer Centre.

Brian Preston and Mark Ebery for the Geography Department, University of Reading, were already using the SPSS package for the analysis of nineteenth-century household returns and had produced a set of forms for the collection of data from the Enumeration books.[6] They kindly provided the author with copies of these forms and they are shown in Figures 1, 2 and 3. (The form for the collection of data from Institutions was not used in this investigation, but is included here for information). The first form is the standard and is completed for all households with data for the head, his wife, children, and other relations and visitors. Details of the total numbers and sex of domestic servants and lodgers is included, and space for details of the first domestic servant is provided. The second sheet records details of the second and subsequent domestics and any lodgers in the household. The address, census and schedule number are written at the top of the sheet, if it is completed, as a precaution against error, and is stapled to the first sheet. If there are second sharing households, a form is completed for these too, the same form as for primary households, but clearly distinguished, and any lodgers or domestic servants they have, recorded on a second sheet. A similar procedure is adopted for any third or subsequent households, and all the sheets for one property are stapled together.

Once the data had been collected for any census, it was coded into a suitable form for computer processing and the keys for the various codes used are given in the Appendix. The coding numbers were first added to the raw data sheet to make checking easier and to highlight any omissions which could be filled by reference back to the Enumeration Books. The coding is of two

3

HEADS FAMILY

Parish	Municipal/parliamentary borough	Town or village	Registration district	Registration sub-district	Enumeration district
Number of household	House number or name	Name of Road or Street			Census

Serial number of household	Serial number of enumeration district	Location coordinates	Number of persons in household	Number in head's household	Type of head	Age of head	Birthplace of head

Social class of head	Industrial group order of head	Age of wife	Birthplace wife	Social class of wife	Industrial group order of wife	Number of children of head	Eldest child of head			
							Age	Sex	Social class	Industrial group order

Child number 2				Child number 3				Child number 4				Child 5		Child 6	
Age	Sex	Social class	Industrial group order	Age	Sex	Social class	Industrial group order	Age	Sex	Social class	Industrial group order	Age	Sex	Age	Sex

Child 7		Child 8		Child 9		Child 10		Number of other relatives of family	Details of 2nd family sharing	Number of lodgers		Number of domestics	
Age	Sex	Age	Sex	Age	Sex	Age	Sex			Female	Male	Female	Male

Number of visitors		Domestic number 1			Workers
Male	Female	Age	Sex	Birthplace	

Figure 1.   The form for the collection of data of the Head's Family.   Note that the details of the first domestic are included on this form.

4

Parish	Municipal/parliamentary borough	Town or village	Registration district	Registration sub-district	Enumeration district
Number of household	House number or name	Name of Road or Street			Census

Serial number of household	Serial number of enumeration district	Domestic number of household	Domestic number 2			Domestic number 3			Domestic number 4		
			Age	Sex	Birthplace	Age	Sex	Birthplace	Age	Sex	Birthplace

Domestic number 5					Lodger number 1					Lodger number 2				
Age	Sex	Birthplace	Social class	Industrial group order	Age	Sex	Birthplace	Social class	Industrial group order	Age	Sex	Birthplace	Social class	Industrial group order

Lodger number 3					Lodger number 4					Lodger number 5		
Age	Sex	Birthplace	Social class	Industrial group order	Age	Sex	Birthplace	Social class	Industrial group order	Age	Sex	Birthplace

Lodger number 5 cont.		Lodger number 6					Lodger number 7				
Social class	Industrial group order	Age	Sex	Birthplace	Social class	Industrial group order	Age	Sex	Birthplace	Social class	Industrial group order

Number of blind

Figure 2. The form for the collection of data of domestics and lodgers. Note that the details of the first domestic are collected on the form for the Head's Family.

INSTITUTIONS

Parish	Municipal/parliamentary borough	Town or Village	Registration district	Registration sub-district	Enumeration district
Number of household	House number or name	Name of Road or Street			Census
Serial number of household	Serial number of enumeration district	Type of institution	Number in institution	Number male	Number female

Age breakdown male

0 - 4	5 - 9	10-19	20-34	35-54	55+

Age breakdown female

0 - 4	5 - 9	10-19	20-34	35-54	55+

Total number of officials

Number of officials	
Male	Female

Numbers in social class

1	2	3	4	5

Figure 3. The form for the collection of data of institutions. (This form was not used and is included here for reference purposes).

6

or three digit numerals, or 'F' and 'M' for sex classification.
The SPSS package provides facilities for sophisticated recoding
of variables and for various ways of treating 'missing information'.
The coding system adopted worked on the principle that where
there was no data for an entry, none was made; for example, if
there were no children in a household, the relevant sections of
the cards were left blank, and the computer 'reads' this as '0',
and these '0's can be included or excluded in the calculations
according to the instructions for controlling the SPSS package.

The coded information was transferred from the data sheets
to computer code sheets. The organisation of information in the
SPSS system is based upon the 'case' with cases grouped together
into 'subfiles', and subfiles grouped together into 'files'. The
case is, therefore, the smallest unit for analysis but can
contain many variables. Eacy property formed one case with the
attributes of the property occupants described by the case
variables. Only minimal information was included about second
and subsequent sharing households, but where these constituted
a significant proportion of the total population each was fully
described on a separate case included in a subfile of sharing
households. Figure 4 shows the construction of the file of the
Wiltshire data and the organisation of cases and subfiles within
it. The File for the Sussex data is simpler as there was an
insignificant proportion of sharing households in Sussex to warrant
their separate investigation. Each case of household data consists
of five computer cards with the one, two or three digital variables
separated by single blanks to make punching and checking easier.
Many of the variables would have no information with them; for
example, a household with no children, so that large parts of many
of the cards contain no punched data. It is possible to ease the
load on the computer by coding the beginning of each blank card

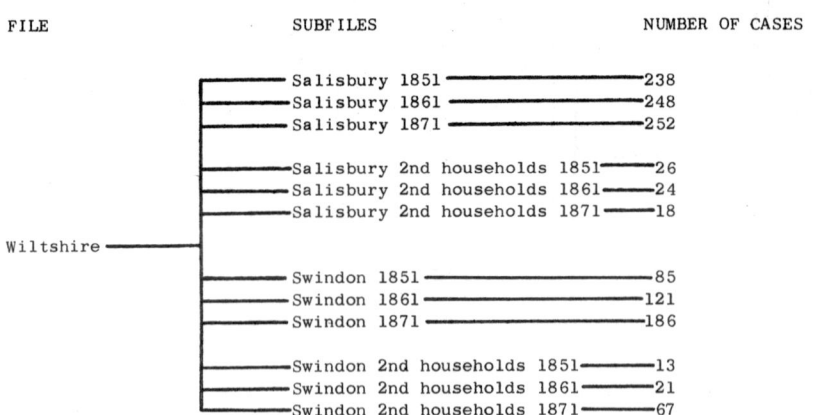

FILE	SUBFILES	NUMBER OF CASES
	Salisbury 1851	238
	Salisbury 1861	248
	Salisbury 1871	252
	Salisbury 2nd households 1851	26
	Salisbury 2nd households 1861	24
	Salisbury 2nd households 1871	18
Wiltshire		
	Swindon 1851	85
	Swindon 1861	121
	Swindon 1871	186
	Swindon 2nd households 1851	13
	Swindon 2nd households 1861	21
	Swindon 2nd households 1871	67

Figure 4.   The file of the Wiltshire data showing the subfile and case
structure.

and writing a separate computer programme to prevent the computer reading the whole card. The computer code sheets and the punched cards were checked, and the SPSS Marginals Routine was found useful for grouping the values of the variables together and identifying those which are outside the likely range. The cards were searched for inaccurate data, and once corrected the data was placed onto a magnetic tape.

The analysis of the data used the SPSS standard routines, although if necessary, special programmes can be written for further analysis. The SPSS package provided various methods of selecting, sorting, weighting, recoding, transforming and creating new variables, and seems admirably suited to this type of investigation.

4. PROVIDING THE SAMPLE

(a) Enumeration District Boundaries

The data for each town at each census was a 10% sample of properties in the towns. The decision on where the data collection boundaries should be drawn was generally determined by the description of the Enumeration District boundaries taken from the Census Books, and only 'whole' Districts were used due to the problems of sub-dividing districts when properties had inadequate addresses. The first edition of the 6 Inches to the Mile maps of the Ordnance Survey was used to plot the boundaries which were then checked with the larger scale 25 Inches to the Mile map series where necessary. In the case of Salisbury for 1861, the top page of each of the Enumeration District Books for the parishes of St. Thomas's and St. Edmund's was missing, so in the absence of a written description the addresses of the properties were used. The Enumeration District written descriptions are of two types. The first starts at one particular building, crossroads of similar feature, and follows the boundary of the District by describing the boundary features in a circuit before returning to the starting point. This was the method adopted in the Horsham and Salisbury books. The second method describes the properties included in the district without concern for a boundary description and this was the method used for Swindon. One of the commonest problems with both methods was the lack of road names and the use of occupants of properties; for example, "...the Eastern Side of Cobb's Lane to Mrs. Smith's inclusive." It is usually possible to estimate the location of such properties with sufficient accuracy for the 6 Inch to the Mile Map from the remainder of the description. However, it is often impossible to locate accurately on the ground any individual property referred to in the Enumerator's books as many urban properties were unnumbered and most rural properties had no number, name or street attached to the description of the household.

The Enumeration District boundaries for each of the ten-year censuses often have similarities in the urban areas of the towns, but were usually very different for the suburban and developing areas. For example, the Enumeration Districts in the centre of Salisbury were similar for each census, while the development of the Fisherton Anger parish required considerable alteration of the boundaries for each census. Swindon and Horsham had similar Enumeration District boundaries at each census in the central area, but differences in the suburban areas. In Swindon, the peculiarities of the New Town, growing by the railway, and its gradual development towards the Old Town on the hill, can be seen by the large size of the Old Town Enumeration Districts compared with the small, compact ones, of the New Town.

(b)   What Constitutes a Household?

At each Census there were written instructions and assistance provided from the Registrars to guide Enumerators in the collection and recording of the household data, including the use of printed sample pages of a completed book, but there was still an enormous variation in the recording of data, and mistakes were often introduced by the checkers and other clerical staff employed to process the books. The identification of individual households, lodgers, and numerous families sharing the same dwelling is never absolutely certain and needs a commonsense approach by the research worker, and a study of the 'style' of the Enumerator to establish his pattern for recording these vital facts. The variety of methods used by Enumerators prevents any set of rules being proposed to guide research workers. The badly damaged condition of some of the books, and the numerous missing pages complicate matters still further and prevent the cross-checking of totals of households. It is apparent that substantial inaccuracies exist where one dwelling was shared by two or more families and the exact division is unclear from the books. Similarly, where tenement buildings existed, as in Swindon, the sharing of accommodation introduces difficulties, or when as in Horsham, where separate families occupied independent dwellings in the back yards of properties, both dwellings had the same number; nor are Enumerators consistent in their approach. The variations in the numbering systems adopted by the Enumerators are legion; sometimes each household is numbered, sometimes each household and each lodger, sometimes everyone described as 'head', but this is often not consistent throughout an Enumeration Book. The book may be numbered throughout beginning at 1, or there may be a collection of runs of numbering each beginning at 1. Often numbers are omitted altogether from a sequence, or numbers are repeated, or individual pages may be numbered. The summary sheets at the beginning of each book are generally fairly accurate counts of dwelling units, households and persons, but these have been checked and altered many times.

(c)   The Sampling Methods

The 10% sample census was selected from each Enumeration District in turn. The total number of dwellings in the District, given in the summary sheet, was checked by a count of the dwellings listed in the book, care being taken to identify any pages photographed twice onto the microfilm, or pages omitted from the sequence and added elsewhere on the film. The numbering schedule of the households was checked to identify the 'style' of the Enumerator, and the treatment of any dwellings which were recorded on two separate pages of the Enumeration Books, as this is a constant source of error.

The method of sampling for Salisbury and Swindon used the total number of dwelling units to calculate the number for a 10% sample, and the dwellings to be sampled were selected with a table of random numbers. The random list was rearranged into numerical sequence and the dwellings in the book counted through until each random number from the list occurred, at which event the details of the household or households were noted. The book was counted through in the order of the household numbering where this was practical, and this is not necessarily the same as the order of pages occurring on the microfilm. If any of the random numbers happened to be an Institution (see below) this was ignored and further random numbers were obtained to make up for any deficiency in the number of dwellings.[9]

The method for sampling in the Horsham case followed Armstrong,[10] where a record was taken of every tenth property in the Enumeration Book; if this was an Institution the eleventh was chosen, and then the ninth afterwards was recorded to maintain the sequence of 'every tenth one'.

FILLING UP THE CENSUS PAPER.

Wife of his Bosom. "UPON MY WORD, MR. PEEWITT! IS THIS THE WAY YOU FILL UP YOUR CENSUS! SO YOU CALL YOURSELF THE 'HEAD OF THE FAMILY'—DO YOU—AND ME A 'FEMALE!'"

5. CLASSIFICATION OF THE DATA AND INTERPRETATION PROCEDURES

(a) The Size of the Household

The three ten-year censuses offer unique details of population structure and urban form, but the interpretation of this data has to be approached with care. The problem of the shared dwelling house has been mentioned above and is described in detail elsewhere.[7] The 1861 census book introduced columns for inhabited houses, and uninhabited and being-built houses, as well as double slashes to indicate the end of the entries to a dwelling house, and a single slash to indicate the end of a household, a great improvement on the 1851 method of indicating single and shared dwellings by the length of the line drawn after the family groups. The totals at the bottom of each page of the books also indicate the number of houses, but with the omission of lines, slashes and a mark in the house column, many different interpretations can be placed upon the relationships between the households. In many instances, the absence of house numbers or addresses to distinguish the separate dwellings further complicates the situation. The instructions to the Enumerators for the 1851 and 1861 censuses differed for the recording of lodgers, boarders and sharing families, and the distinctions were never fully understood or consistently applied. In 1861, single male lodgers were often recorded as occupying shared houses, but were given a relationship of lodger to the head of the household. The distinction between lodgers who rented accommodation, either floors or rooms of dwellings for their exclusive use, and boarders who shared accommodation with the occupying family is lost. The problems of identifying separate family units who rented accommodation for their exclusive use and did their own cooking, and the son-in-law and family living with the head of the household are both often impossible to identify under the title 'lodger'. The overall confusion can be demonstrated by the use of the terms boarder and lodger by the Enumerators for sometimes only one of the terms is used throughout a book, sometimes the term 'boarder' is used solely for children, and in other cases there would seem to be no pattern at all. It is likely that this confusion results in serious errors in the results where individuals are treated as separate sharing households.

(b) Property Addresses

Once the numbers of households in each sampled property had been found, the schedule number and address of the property were recorded, although often the address consisted of only the street or road name, or name of that part of the town. For most of Swindon and Salisbury, full addresses were used and provided a detailed guide to the occupancy of dwellings in the town. The names of a number of roads and streets have changed since the early censuses (for example, Grub Street, Horsham, became Highland Avenue), so early Ordnance Survey maps were required to find the roads mentioned, or to identify the full extent of the road as it was originally, where a part of it had since been renamed (for example, in Wimblehurst Road, Horsham). The actual system of numbering the individual dwellings may have altered over

11

the years to cater for the introduction of new dwellings into a
road, so special care is needed to identify, on the ground, the
dwellings detailed in the census.

(c) Household 'Heads'

For the purpose of this research, the most important person
in the household is the one described as 'head', and the overall
household classifications follow from this. There is a large
amount of variation between households which are similar in other
respects, but have 'heads' with different characteristics. The
widowed mother, whose occupation is given as 'supported by her
children' can be compared with the 75-year-old female head of a
Salisbury family whose occupation is 'butcher'. In the first
example, the eldest son is the head; in the second example, the
eldest son remains the eldest son. The previous fortunes of the
family and the characteristics of the members obviously determines
who is the 'head', but for the purpose of this analysis different
results, due to this classification, are obtained for groups of
people who would otherwise be considered similar. The head of
the household is classified according to the sex, marital status,
presence or absence of his or her children within the household,
and by the use of 'head equivalents' when the normal head is away
from home on the night of the census. A list of the types of head
and head equivalents used is given in Appendix 1. A particular
problem in comparing the three towns is the significant number of
illegitimate children living in Salisbury with their mothers.
These have been classified as such, but why this feature is not
apparent in Swindon or Horsham is impossible to say.[11] Perhaps
the Enumerators in Salisbury had personal knowledge of the families
and they could not conceal themselves as 'widow' or 'married woman
with children'.

(d) Children in the Household

In general terms, there are numerous errors to be found
throughout all the censuses where children in households are
described as 'son' or 'daughter' particularly when the head and
his wife are either too old or too young for such a relationship.
These children have been classified throughout as 'other relatives
of the family' and the head classified according to the remaining
household characteristics. A similar situation exists with the
confusing use of the terms 'son-in-law' for 'step-son' and
üaughter-in-law' for 'step-daughter', and here again evidence of
surnames may assist, but if the person is an adult it may still be
uncertain whether or not the 'son-in-law' is a child of the head
of the household.

(e) The Recording of Ages

The age of the head of the household, and the age of all the
people in the books are rarely omitted. When a person was unsure
it is probable that the Enumerators made a guess, and examples
exist where Enumerators left the age blank and the census checkers
have added an age guess based upon the remainder of the information
available. Checks on the accuracy of the ages stated by the same

people at each of the three censuses seem to be satisfactory,[7] and such accuracy is certainly adequate for the five-year age bands used in this study and given in the Appendix.

(f) The Recording of Birthplace

The birthplace of the people listed in the Enumeration Books are given by Parish and County in England, and usually by Wales, Scotland, or Ireland alone for these countries. People born abroad are usually described only by country, but often with 'A British Citizen' added. A lack of geographical skill is apparent for many enumerators who, for example, placed Birmingham freely in a number of Midland counties, or phonetically spelled the names of other towns. For those people in Salisbury, Swindon and Horsham who were born in the home county, details have been recorded of the parish to provide information on migration, but it is often impossible to accurately identify their village of origin. For example, there are five 'Charltons' and two 'Bishopstones' in Wiltshire, and in Sussex, an Upper and Lower Beeding many miles apart, to allocate all those people born in 'Beeding'. An intimate knowledge of the counties is useful to identify those hamlets or even crossroads given as places of origin by the residents of the three towns, but it is apparent that many of these may be attributed wrongly. For residents of the three towns born outside the county, the information is collected on the basis of the county, with a check where necessary to confirm the location of a town if one is quoted. The Appendix gives a list of the county classification, and special attention should be taken of emigrants from London who are subdivided into Middlesex London and Surrey London, with the emigrants from the City of London placed into the Middlesex London category.

(g) The Recording of Occupation

The occupation details of the head of the household, the wife of the head, the head's children, and all lodgers were extracted and classified, and which, together with details of domestic servants, enables an occupation and social class comparison, at the three censuses, for each of the three towns. The occupation classification follows the work of Armstrong[3] and is described in detail in the Appendix. The main sources of inaccuracy are as follows:

(1) The term 'annuitant' is often used in the occupation column, with no further indication of the previous occupation or current social class and without such further information it is impossible to accurately classify the person. For example, an annuitant occupying an almshouse might be evidence of a Social Class rating of V, the lowest, whereas the presence of domestic servants might indicate a Social Class I or II household but for many annuitants no such evidence exists. Occasionally, the occupation is given as 'proprietor of houses' or similar phrase giving an indication of possible wealth, although it does not say how much property. The classification method adopted in cases where the information is inadequate for a clear inclusion in a social class was to place the person in social class II, and this may well overweight the importance of this class in the study.

13

(2)   Classification of household occupation and social class
according to the characteristics of the head of the household
overlooks the characteristics of the remaining members of the
households, and although details of the remaining members can
easily be produced, all the major analyses of data is solely on
the basis of the head's characteristics. One of the more important
errors this introduces concerned the schoolmistress, who is placed
in Social Class II, but is married to an agricultural worker of
Social Class IV. Surprisingly, there were a number of such cases
in the study data.

(3)   This survey has concentrated on the households and has not
considered Institutions. The census returns for the Work Houses
contain many destitute people who, if they were in households,
would affect the overall results of this work. The ages of the
Work House occupants seem, from a cursory view, to be evenly
spread and not concentrated among the old. The Lunatic Asylums
and Infirmaries again contain wide cross-sections of the population
of the towns. A number of paupers were collected by the 10%
sample where they were living as heads of households or within a
household, and were usually described in the occupation column
as 'paupers supported by the parish'.

(4)   The classification of a tradesman as 'master' was considered
insufficient on its own to place him in a social class above the
normal 'journeyman' tradesman. If, however, there were domestic
servants, or apprentices and lodgers in the household described
as journeyman, this was taken as sufficient evidence to place the
master in the higher social class. For example, a journeyman
shoemaker would be classified as Social Class III, whereas a
master shoemaker who met the requirements listed above would be
placed in Social Class II.

(5)   Landlords of beerhouses, hotels and licensed premises were
generally classified in Social Class III unless they had domestic
servants who did not work as barmaids, ostlers or liveried
servants, or had a number of adult daughters with no occupation
listed, or other indication of wealth, when they would be placed
in Social Class II.

(6)   Apprentices generally were given a Social Class of IV if
the trade or profession was within Social Class II or III. Pupil
teachers were therefore considered as IV, and so were apprentice
plumbers. With some trades, where a different level of skill
exists, these were classified in different social classes. For
example, a 'tailoress' would be Social Class III, but a needle-
woman or seamstress placed in Social Class IV, and similarly a
blacksmith given Class III but a hammerman as Social Class IV.

(7)   The problem of economic recession or changes in the types
of trade have effects which are reflected in the social classification. In Salisbury a number of pauper flannel makers appeared
and were entered in Social Class V and not Social Class III.

(8)   People who are described as unemployed were placed in the
Social Class according to their occupation; for example,
'unemployed bricklayer' in Class III, and this classification,
like modern systems of classifying occupation, is not a measure
of wealth.

(9) Many of the current social measures of wealth and class are inadequate to consider the nineteenth century situation in these towns. The family with domestic servants living-in can be of high social class, but may also be headed by a Class IV agricultural worker, or consist of a father and sons of Social Class V general labourers. When a parent was widowed it is common to find a living-in domestic employed, and many families had domestic services provided by neices or relations from the country living in the household and described as 'domestic servant at home'.

(10) The division of the town into good quality, working class, and slum areas was certainly not possible in Salisbury and Horsham, and although the New Town of Swindon was almost entirely occupied by employees of the railway works, the Old Town was a social mixture. This prevents the easy social classification of the population using the home address as a guide, as is possible in many of the United Kingdom towns today. In Horsham it was common for the occupants of large houses with substantial grounds to live next door to a terrace of cottages occupied by people from all social classes. In Swindon and Salisbury, the number of households with lodgers and the resulting mixture of social classes prevented the physical division of the town on the lines of social class.

The occupation and social class of the wife of the head of the household was recorded when such entries occurred in the census books. Most wives were solely occupied with household duties and no separate employment was listed. Of those who had occupations most worked in connection with the family business; for example, milliners, tailoresses or seamstresses when their husbands were listed as tailors. Apart from these, the most common types of female employment were as domestic servants, washerwomen or laundresses.

The occupation and social class of the children of the head of the household were recorded for the five oldest children (and the age and sex up to a maximum of ten children). The description of a child as 'scholar' was recorded and they were generally three years or older; for those children younger than three years any scholar description has been ignored. The order of the children listed in the Enumeration Books was, where necessary, rearranged so that they are classified in descending age order. (The Enumeration Books sometimes listed children in terms of males first, or children of current marriage followed by step children of either or both spouses, or occasionally just a list with no obvious order at all). There are often discrepancies in the sex attributed to children where their age is placed incorrectly in the Male or Female column of the books. For classification purposes, the evidence of Christian name determined the sex.

(h)   The Size of the Families

The census information does not, of course, give a complete view of the family, but only the structure of the households on the census night, and although the size of the family on this night is given, the total number of children of the parents of any household is unknown. Indeed, the very large number of living-in domestic servants under the age of sixteen indicates

that for many of the children, especially females, family life
only lasted for about fourteen years until they left home. It
is impossible, therefore, to produce details of the average number
of children per marriage without reference to other contemporary
reference sources. The size of the families is further distorted
by the job opportunities available to teenage males, as to whether
they took a similar employment to their father and lived at home
or took employment as an apprentice and lived away from home. The
figures available from the census provide raw data on family size
at a point in time and although they may stimulate many hypotheses
as to the reasons for the family characteristics, they provide no
proof.

     Many families in Social Group I or II did not state occupations
for their adult daughters living at home, and a measure of high
social class can be inferred from this. The sons of Social Class
I and II families often followed their father into the Law, the
professions, or the armed forces and were not, therefore, at
home on census night. The Close, in Salisbury, provides an
interesting enclave of higher social class households where the
pattern of child upbringing and occupation can be studied. In
each of the towns a number of schools occur where children boarded
and these were classed as Institutions and were omitted from
this study, but of course this does distort the overall features
of the population of the towns revealed by the study.

     The New Town at Swindon offers interesting insights into the
formation and growth of families, as many of the residents were
young, just starting families, and the physical growth of the new
buildings and the full addresses used, enables the family structure
to be studied on a house by house basis. At a superficial
inspection, the average age of the head of the household, the
small average size of the families, the relative absence of old
people, and the skilled manual occupation of the head provide a
similarity with the occupants of the post World War II New Towns
in the United Kingdom.

     In each of the three towns, a number of the families in the
10% sample had children living in the household although they
were not the issue of the head. The classification treated these
children in one of three ways. If they were described as visitors
they were classified as such; if they were described as boarder
and, from the name and age details, seemed to have no blood
relation to the household, they were treated as lodgers, and if
they were a relation of the head of the household they were
classified as 'other relatives of the household'. The most common
'extra' children in households were grandchildren, living either
with or without their parents, followed by nephews, neices and
cousins. If these children were teenagers they often had occupations, but these were omitted from the study in the 'other relatives
of the household' category. The problem of the numbers of illegitimate children in Salisbury has already been mentioned above.

(i) Domestic Servants

     Domestic servants can be divided into six categories, initially
by sex, and then each sex subdivided by whether they lived at
home, or at their place of work. Only the larger households with

16

heads of high social class seemed to employ male servants.
Among the female servants, various grades can be distinguished
such as Housekeeper, Cook, Domestic servant, and Childminder,
but these descriptions in the Enumeration Books do not reflect
the numerous types of servants which occurred in practice.
The age of the servant seems to offer a guide to her ability
and the list of servants in the books is usually in order of
importance. Many of the young women who were born and lived in
each of the three towns worked locally as domestic servants, and
either lived at home or lived-in at their place of work. Other
domestics came from the surrounding villages and usually lived in
or occasionally lodged in the town, while other domestics often
came from distant counties. Here, a pattern is evident as employers
sought domestics in their home village, and a household could exist,
in say, Salisbury, where the head, his wife and two domestics all
came from the same East Anglian village, whereas all the children
were born in Salisbury.

The most common form of domestic employment was for a single
female between the ages of 12 and 16 in a household, and this was
true for all three towns. Even families of low social class had
domestic servants, and domestics were commonly employed in households where there were numerous lodgers. The number of female
domestics in the 20 years and over age group rapidly diminished,
presumably due to marriage, and the few middle-aged domestics
were generally styled as housekeepers or cooks. The classification
system adopted for domestic staff was age, sex, and birthplace,
for those staff who lived in, and for those who lived apart from
their work, age, sex, birthplace, occupation and social class.

(j) Lodgers

The data extracted from the census for lodgers followed a
similar pattern to that for the head of the household: age, sex,
place of birth, occupation, and social class were recorded. Those
persons excluded from the lodger classification were:

(1) Members of the same family as the head of the household.
For example, a nephew of the household head living in a family
where all the males had their occupation described as 'butcher',
was classified as 'other member of the family'. The simplicity
of the coding of this latter category omits the nephew from any
occupation and social class statistics. Grandchildren and
mothers-in-law were similarly placed in the 'other relative of the
family' category.

(2) Persons who could be classified under domestic servant. For
example, on a farm, a number of males and females may be described
as lodgers in their relation to the head of the household, but
those whose duties were primarily domestic were classified as
such. (The agricultural labourers would be classified as lodgers).

The lodgers in a town form an important category and a
significant part of the total workforce. Many of the lodgers in
a household followed the same occupation as the head or sons of
the household and many masters had their journeyman employees
lodging with them. The situation in the New Town of Swindon was

especially marked, with many lodgers coming from the same town as their landlords and following similar trades in the railway factories. It can be assumed from the data that many households considered lodgers as a prime source of income and had many staying at one time. The public houses also housed lodgers, but many of these people were following itinerent occupations.

The classification, lodger, has already been mentioned as a problem in deciding which should be more properly considered as sharing households in their own right with their own heads, and the fact that some of the lodgers have their own domestic servants further complicates matters. No rigidly applied rules were developed for placing the 'lodger' in the lodger or sharing households category, but each case was considered on its merits and the style of the Enumerator carefully studied for guidance. Significant errors may have been introduced in the classification and use of this data.

The lodgers are of all social classes, many different occupations, and the society presumably accepted lodging as a normal method of providing accommodation with no social stigma attached to it. There seems to be no relationship between the social groups who lodged and those with whom they stayed, a general mixture of occupations and social groups is apparent. The most common lodger was a single male, although single female lodgers occurred but these were rarer, and occasionally whole families were described as lodgers in households where this may be a true classification. For example, in a list of ten lodgers at a property, four of them can be considered a husband, wife and two children from their names and ages, although all ten were described as lodgers.

An important qualification to the results regarding lodgers published here concerns those who lived at their place of work. An example is the Draper's shop where the household head, his family and domestics had thirteen young females living with them and employed as shop assistants. Similar cases of male shop assistants employed by chemists occurred and these assistants have been classified as lodgers on the premises and placed within the appropriate occupation group. Providing lodgings for employees seems to have been a normal method for shopkeepers to provide themselves with staff, and is obviously a significant opportunity for employment, so they have been included in the data, although some bias in the overall results may result.

(k) Shared Properties

This study assumes that where two or more households share the same property, the order of the households in the Enumeration Books is a guide to their relative importance; the dominant household coming first, and the subsidiary household second. Such assumptions may well be unwarranted, for the property may well be owned by a landlord who lived elsewhere and who let it to two separate households, so that the position in the books meant very little. However, for the purposes of this study, second and subsequent sharing households have been grouped together for further analysis.[12]

There are significant numbers of sharing households in Salisbury and Swindon for each of the three censuses, but insignificant sharing households in Horsham, which has, therefore, been omitted from this part of the study. The sharing of properties and how this changed over time is assumed to be important to measures of housing demand, housing supply, and job opportunities. The second sharing household may be of more recent immigration to the town than the dominant household, and the age of the family members, their occupation and counties of origin may give an indication of the relative attractions of the town at the time. In fact, the analysis of the data of the sharing households does show particular characteristics common between the households, and for the New Town area of Swindon an especially interesting pattern of immigration and house sharing emerges. The data given in the tables indicate the number of shared properties in the towns at each census and the details of the sharing families are classified in the same way as the details of the dominant households. Some of the properties may have three or more sharing families, but these were usually where two or more single people were listed as 'head' in the enumeration lists.

REFERENCES

1. The methods of selecting the samples of properties are described later in the paper and criticisms of one of the methods are to be found in reference 9.

2. For example, the work of W.A. Armstrong for York is not comparable: Armstrong, W.A. (1967), The Social Structure of York 1841-51: An Essay in Quantified History, Ph.D. Thesis, University of Birmingham.

3. The coding for occupation and social class follows, with two minor additions, the method of classification of Armstrong, W.A. (1972), The use of information about occupation, in Wrigley, E.A. (ed), Nineteenth Century Society, Cambridge University Press, Chapter 6, Appendices A and E, pp.215-223 and 284-310.

4. A fuller description of the process of collection of National Census Returns can be found in Drake, M. (1972), The census, 1801-1891, in Wrigley, E.A. op.cit., Chapter 1, pp.7-46, and Taylor, A.J. (1951), The taking of the census, 1801-1951, British Medical Journal, April 7, Vol. 1, pp.715-720, and HMSO Guide to Official Sources No. 2, Census Report of Great Britain, 1801-1931.

5. Wrigley, E.A. (ed) (1966). An Introduction to English Historical Demography, London, Weidenfeld and Nicolson, and Wrigley, E.A. (ed) (1972), op.cit.

6. Recent work at the Department of Geography, University of Reading by Brian Preston on family structure in nineteenth century England and the provision of local government services in urban areas, and by Mark Ebery for the town of Reading, Berkshire, and a number of post graduate students at the Department of Economic History, University of Leicester. See also the recent study of domestic servants by Ebery, M. and Preston, B. (1976), Domestic Service in Late Victorian and Edwardian England, 1871-1914, Geographical Paper No. 42, University of Reading, and the forthcoming study on occupations of father and son by Preston, B. (1977), Occupations of Father and Son in Mid-Victorian England, Geographical Paper No. 56, Department of Geography, University of Reading.

7. The most useful reference on the accuracy of the nineteenth century census returns is Tillott, P.M. (1972), Sources of inaccuracy in the 1851 and 1861 censuses, in Wrigley, E.A., op.cit., pp.82-133.

8. Nie, N.H., Hull, C.H., Jenkins, J.G., Steinbrenner, K. and Bent, D.H. (1975), Statistical Package for the Social Sciences (2nd Edition), New York, McGraw-Hill.

9. For a general discussion on sampling methods see Schofield, R.S. (1972), in Wrigley, E.A. op.cit., Chapter 5, pp.146-190.

10. Armstrong, W.A. (1966), Social structure from the early census returns, in Wrigley, E.A. (ed), op.cit., but also see the criticisms of this method in Floud, R.C. and Schofield, R.S. (1968), Social structure from the early census returns, a comment, Economic History Review, Vol. 21, pp.607-609, and

Armstrong, W.A. (1968), Rejoinder, Economic History Review, ibid., pp.609-613.

11. Compare this with Anderson, M. (1972), The study of family structure, in Wrigley, E.A., op.cit., Chapter 2, pp.47-81, reference on page 66 to the illegitimate children encountered in the Preston, Lancashire study.

12. See Figure 4 for the subfile structure of the census data and the files for second households.

DEFINITIONS

Primary and Secondary Households

The tables are divided into those for primary and those for secondary households. The primary households consists of one household from each inhabited property in the 10% sample of the town. The secondary households include details of the remainder of the households in the inhabited property in the 10% sample of the town. For example, in a house occupied by four families, one family would occur on the primary list, and the other three would occur on the secondary household list. In the 'table for the number of persons in secondary households in each dwelling unit', the total number of persons in the three secondary households is used.

Type of Household Head

The types of household head are classified as follows and abbreviations are provided in the tables. The presence or absence of children in the household is a reference only to children of the head and/or the wife. Visiting children, grandchildren or other children present are not used for the 'type of head' classification.

Type of household head:

Male unmarried with no children present
Male married
Male married with children present
Female unmarried with no children present
Widower with no children present
Widower with children present
Widow with no children present
Widow with children present
Head absent
Child (includes all offspring of parents, not only infants)
Female unmarried with children present
Female married with children present
Brother of head
Domestic servant of head
Lodger of head

Industrial Groups and Social Classes

The arrangement of Industrial Groups and Social Classes in the following tables follows the method of Armstrong, W.A. (1972) The use of information about occupation, in Wrigley, E.A. (ed), Nineteenth Century Society, Cambridge University Press, pp.215-223 and 284-310, apart from the following alterations for industrial groups:

(a) 'Building 3: Roadmaking' has been divided into:

Building - Roadmaking: excavator, navvy, pavior, road
labourer.
and   Railway making: railway plate layer, railway
labourer.

(b) 'Manufacturer 15: Carriages and harness' has been divided
    into:

    Manufacture 15: Carriages and harness:
                    Axletree maker, coachmaker, others connected
                    with carriages, perambulator, wheel chair
                    maker, saddle harness manufacturer, wheel-
                    wright, whip maker.

    and   Railway carriage spring/buffer maker,
                    railway carriage, wagon maker, railway
                    wheel maker.

(c) The addition of a classification 'scholar'.

    The following lists the occupations as classified in
Armstrong's study (see above reference) .and
used in the following tables. Only the main headings are listed.

Occupation Group

AGRICULTURE AND BREEDING
    1. Farming
    2. Land service
    3. Breeding
    4. Fishing
MINING
    1. Mining
    2. Quarrying
    3. Brickmaking
    4. Salt and waterworks
BUILDING
    1. Management
    2. Operative
    3. Roadmaking
       (railway making)
MANUFACTURE
    1. Machinery
    2. Tools, etc.
    3. Shipbuilding
    4. Iron and steel
    5. Copper, tin, lead, etc.
    6. Gold and silver
    7. Earthenware
    8. Coals and gas
    9. Chemicals
    10. Furs and leather
    11. Glue, tallow, etc.
    12. Hair, etc.
    13. Woodworkers
    14. Furniture
    15. Carriages and harness
        (railway carriage, etc.)
    16. Paper
    17. Floorcloth, waterproofs, etc.
    18. Woollens
    19. Cotton and silk
    20. Flax, hemp, etc.
    21. Lace
    22. Dyeing
    23. Dress

24. Sundries
25. Food preparation
26. Baking
27. Drink preparation
28. Smoking
29. Watches, instruments, toys, etc.
30. Printing
31. Unspecified
TRANSPORT
1. Warehouses and docks
2. Ocean navigation
3. Inland navigation
4. Railways
5. Roads
DEALING
1. Coals
2. Raw materials
3. Clothing materials
4. Dress
5. Food
6. Tobacco
7. Wines, spirits, hotels
8. Lodging and coffee houses
9. Furniture
10. Stationery and publications
11. Household utensils, ornaments
12. General dealers
13. Unspecified
INDUSTRIAL SERVICE
1. Banking, insurance, accountancy
2. General labourers
PUBLIC SERVICE AND PROFESSIONAL
1. Central administration
2. Local administration
3. Sanitary administration
4. Army
5. Navy
6. Police and prisons
7. Law
8. Medicine
9. Art and amusement (painting)
10. Art and amusement (music, etc.)
11. Literature
12. Science
13. Education
14. Religion
DOMESTIC SERVICE
1. Indoor
2. Outdoor
3. Extra service
PROPERTY OWNING AND INDEPENDENT
SCHOLAR

Birthplace Classification

By study town, county or country:

Horsham
Sussex except Horsham
Swindon
Salisbury

Wiltshire except Swindon and Salisbury
Fareham
Gosport
Hampshire except Fareham and Gosport
Kent
Surrey
Surrey London
Middlesex London
Middlesex
Dorset
Somerset
Devonshire
Cornwall
Monmouthshire
Gloucestershire
Berkshire
Oxfordshire
Buckinghamshire
Bedfordshire
Huntfordshire
Essex
Suffolk
Norfolk
Cambridgeshire
Huntingdonshire
Northamptonshire
Warwickshire
Worcestershire
Herefordshire
Shropshire
Staffordshire
Leicestershire
Rutland
Lincolnshire

Nottinghamshire
Derbyshire
Cheshire
Lancashire
Yorkshire
Westmoreland
Cumberland
Durham
Northumberland
Channel Islands
Wales
Ireland
Scotland
France
Isle of Man
Switzerland
Holland
East Indies
Persia
Germany
West Indies
Africa
America
Unknown

INDEX TO THE TABLES

Town 1: Horsham. Primary households, 1851, 1861 and 1871.

Horsham. Secondary households, 1851, 1861 and 1871.

No significant number

Swindon.   Comparison of New and Old Swindon, primary
           households in 1871.

Table 60   Size
      61   Type of head
      62   Age of head
      63   Birthplace of head
      64   Social class of head
      65   Industrial group of head
      66   Number of children of head and/or wife
      67   Number of domestic servants
      68   Number of lodgers
      69   Number of persons in secondary households

NOTE

    The tables for Horsham include 10% of all properties in
Enumeration Districts described as part of "the town of Horsham"
and omit the rural parts of the parish. The tables for Swindon
include 10? of all properties in the parish. The tables for
Salisbury include 10% of all properties in the parishes of
St. Thomas, St. Martin, St. Edmund, Fisherton Anger, and the
Liberty of the Close.

Table 1. Size of primary households in Horsham: 1851, 1861 and 1871 (10% sample)

Number of persons in family	Number of households of each type					
	1851		1861		1871	
	Freq	%	Freq	%	Freq	%
1	3	5.3	2	2.6	5	5.1
2	11	19.3	8	10.5	17	17.3
3	9	15.8	10	13.2	11	11.2
4	8	14.0	19	25.0	16	16.3
5	6	10.5	9	11.8	21	21.4
6	8	14.0	8	10.5	10	10.2
7	2	3.5	9	11.8	8	8.2
8	2	3.5	3	3.9	4	4.1
9	2	3.5	4	5.3	2	2.0
10	2	3.5	3	3.9	1	1.0
11	2	3.5	-	-	-	-
12	-	-	-	-	1	1.0
13	1	1.8	1	1.3	1	1.0
14	1	1.8	-	-	1	1.0
Total	57	100.0	76	100.0	98	100.0

Table 2. Type of head of primary households in Horsham: 1851, 1861 and 1871 (10% sample)

Type of head of household						
Male unmarried, no children	1	1.8	3	3.9	5	5.1
Mald married, no children	9	15.8	6	7.9	19	19.4
Male married, children	32	56.1	43	56.6	52	53.1
Female unmarried, no children	3	5.3	5	6.6	5	5.1
Widower, no children	1	1.8	1	1.3	2	2.0
Widower, children	4	7.0	4	5.3	2	2.0
Widow, no children	4	7.0	1	1.3	3	3.1
Widow, children	2	3.5	9	11.8	8	8.2
Head absent	-	-	-	-	1	1.0
Female unmarriea, children	-	-	1	1.3	1	1.0
Female married, children	1	1.8	1	1.3		
Brother	-	-	1	1.3	-	-
Domestic servant	-	-.	1	1.3	-	-
Total	57	100.0	76	100.0	98	100.0

Table 3. Age of head of primary households in Horsham: 1851, 1861 and 1871 (10% sample)

Age of head of household	1851 Freq	1851 %	1861 Freq	1861 %	1871 Freq	1871 %
20-24	2	3.5	3	3.9	4	4.1
25-29	3	5.3	7	9.2	11	11.2
30-34	3	5.3	11	14.5	10	10.2
35-39	6	10.5	11	14.5	16	16.3
40-44	9	15.8	11	14.5	5	5.1
45-49	7	12.3	8	10.5	12	12.2
50-54	7	12.3	5	6.6	9	9.2
55-59	7	12.3	9	11.8	10	10.2
60-64	4	7.0	3	3.9	9	9.2
65-69	2	3.5	3	3.9	6	6.1
70-74	5	8.8	3	3.9	4	4.1
75-79	1	1.8	1	1.3	1	1.0
80-84	1	1.8	1	1.3	-	-
Missing values	-	-	-	-	1	1.0
Total	57	100.0	76	100.0	98	100.0

Table 4. Birthplace of head of primary households in Horsham: 1851, 1861 and 1871 (10% sample)

Birthplace of head of household	1851 Freq	1851 %	1861 Freq	1861 %	1871 Freq	1871 %
Horsham	26	45.6	33	43.4	34	34.7
Sussex except Horsham	17	29.8	30	39.5	29	29.6
Wilts except Salisbury & Swindon	-	-	-	-	1	1.0
Hampshire	-	-	-	-	5	5.1
Kent	-	-	2	2.6	3	3.1
Surrey	5	8.8	3	3.9	11	11.2
Surrey.London	1	1.8	-	-	1	1.0
Middlesex London	1	1.8	2	2.6	3	3.1
Middlesex	1	1.8	1	1.3	1	1.0
Dorset	1	1.8	1	1.3	-	-
Somerset	1	1.8	-	-	-	-
Gloucestershire	-	-	1	1.3	-	-
Oxfordshire	-	-	-	-	1	1.0
Buckinghamshire	-	-	1	1.3	-	-
Bedfordshire	1	1.8	-	-	-	-
Essex	-	-	-	-	1	1.0
Suffolk	-	-	-	-	1	1.0
Norfolk	1	1.8	-	-	-	-
Cambridgeshire	-	-	-	-	1	1.0
Huntingdonshire	1	1.8	-	-	-	-
Yorkshire	-	-	-	-	1	1.0
Wales	-	-	1	1.3	1	1.0
Scotland	-	-	-	-	2	2.0
East Indies	1	1.8	1	1.3	-	-
Missing values	-	-	-	-	2	2.0
Totals	57	100.0	76	100.0	98	100.0

Table 5. Social class of head of primary households in Horsham: 1851, 1861 and 1871 (10% sample)

| | Number of households of each type | | | | | |
| | 1851 | | 1861 | | 1871 | |
Social class	Freq	%	Freq	%	Freq	%
1	2	3.5	7	9.2	10	10.2
2	21	36.8	14	18.4	18	18.4
3	21	36.8	31	40.8	37	37.8
4	10	17.5	12	15.8	14	14.3
5	3	5.3	9	11.8	10	10.2
Missing values	-	-	3	3.9	9	9.2
Totals	57	100.0	76	100.0	98	100.0

Table 6. Industrial group of head of primary households in Horsham: 1851, 1861 and 1871 (10% sample)

Industrial group						
Agriculture and Breeding						
Farming	6	10.5	5	6.6	11	11.2
Breeding	1	1.8	-	-	1	1.0
Mining						
Brickmaking	-	-	1	1.3	-	-
Building						
Management	1	1.8	-	-	3	3.1
Operative	6	10.5	12	15.8	8	8.2
Railways	-	-	1	1.3	1	1.0
Manufacture						
Iron and steel	2	3.5	3	3.9	1	1.0
Coals and gas	1	1.8	-	-	-	-
Chemicals	-	-	1	1.3	-	-
Glue, tallow, etc.	1	1.8	-	-	-	-
Woodworkers	1	1.8	2	2.6	2	2.0
Furniture	1	1.8	2	2.6	1	1.0
Carriages and harness	3	5.3	1	1.3	1	1.0
Flax, hemp, etc.	-	-	1	1.3	-	-
Dress	6	10.5	10	13.2	16	16.3
Food preparation	-	-	2	2.6	1	1.0
Baking	-	-	-	-	2	2.0
Drink preparation	-	-	3	3.9	1	1.0
Smoking	-	-	1	1.3	-	-
Watches, instruments, etc.	-	-	1	1.3	-	-
Unspecified	-	-	-	-	1	1.0
Transport						
Warehouses and docks	-	-	1	1.3	-	-
Railways	-	-	-	-	2	2.0
Roads	2	3.5	1	1.3	3	3.1
Dealing						
Raw materials	1	1.8	-	-	1	1.0
Clothing materials	-	-	-	-	1	1.0
Dress	1	1.8	1	1.3	-	-
Food	1	1.8	2	2.6	2	2.0
Wines, spirits, hotels	3	5.3	-	-	5	5.1
Stationery and publications	-	-	1	1.3	2	2.0
Household utensils	1	1.8	1	1.3	-	-
Unspecified	1	1.8	-	-	1	1.0

Table 6 (Continued)

Industrial group	1851 Freq	%	1861 Freq	%	1871 Freq	%
			Number of households of each type			
			1851	1861	1871	
Industrial Service						
Banking, insurance, etc.	2	3.5	–	–	–	–
General labourers	2	3.5	3	3.9	7	7.1
Public Service and Professional						
Central administration	–	–	–	–	1	1.0
Army	–	–	–	–	2	2.0
Law	2	3.5	–	–	–	–
Medicine	–	–	2	2.6	1	1.0
Education	–	–	1	1.3	1	1.0
Religion	–	–	–	–	2	2.0
Domestic Service.						
Indoor	1	1.8	2	2.6	–	–
Outdoor	–	–	2	2.6	1	1.0
Extra service	3	5.3	3	3.9	1	1.0
Property Owning and Independent	7	12.3	6	7.9	6	6.1
Missing values	1	1.8	4	5.3	9	9.2
Totals	57	100.0	76	100.0	98	100.0

Table 7. Age of wife of head of primary households in Horsham: 1851, 1861 and 1871 (10% sample)

Age of wife	Freq	%	Freq	%	Freq	%
20-24	2	3.5	8	10.5	7	7.1
25-29	6	10.5	5	6.6	10	10.2
30-34	6	10.5	8	10.5	9	9.2
35-39	3	5.3	9	11.8	7	7.1
40-44	7	12.3	6	7.9	9	9.2
45-49	7	12.3	7	9.2	11	11.2
50-54	3	5.3	2	2.6	8	8.2
55-59	3	5.3	1	1.3	3	3.1
60-64	1	1.8	–	–	3	3.1
65-69	1	1.8	1	1.3	1	1.0
70-74	1	1.8	–	–	1	1.0
75-79	–	–	–	–	1	1.0
Missing values	17	29.8	29	38.2	28	28.6
Totals	57	100.0	76	100.0	98	100.0

Table 8. Birthplace of wife of head of primary households
in Horsham: 1851, 1861 and 1871 (10% sample)

| | Number of households of each type | | | | | |
| | 1851 | | 1861 | | 1871 | |
Birthplace of wife	Freq	%	Freq	%	Freq	%
Horsham	17	29.8	17	22.4	21	21.4
Sussex except Horsham	14	24.6	19	25.0	24	24.5
Hampshire	1	1.8	-	-	2	2.0
Kent	-	-	2	2.6	2	2.0
Surrey	2	3.5	2	2.6	3	3.1
Surrey London	1	1.8	1	1.3	1	1.0
Middlesex London	1	1.8	1	1.3	4	4.1
Middlesex	-	-	1	1.3	4	4.1
Somerset	-	-	1	1.3	1	1.0
Berkshire	-	-	-	-	1	1.0
Buckinghamshire	-	-	1	1.3	1	1.0
Suffolk	-	-	-	-	2	2.0
Norfolk	1	1.8	-	-	-	-
Northamptonshire	-	-	1	1.3	-	-
Lincolnshire	-	-	-	-	1	1.0
Yorkshire	-	-	-	-	1	1.0
Channel Islands	-	-	-	-	1	1.0
Scotland	-	-	-	-	1	1.0
Missing values	20	35.1	30	39.5	28	28.6
Totals	57	100.0	76	100.0	98	100.0

Table 9. Number of children of the head and/or wife in the
primary households in Horsham: 1851, 1861 and 1871
(10% sample)

Number of children						
1	15	26.3	16	21.1	14	14.3
2	4	7.0	11	14.5	17	17.3
3	5	8.8	8	10.5	15	15.3
4	6	10.5	9	11.8	9	9.2
5	4	7.0	8	10.5	4	4.1
6	1	1.8	2	2.6	2	2.0
7	3	5.3	1	1.3	3	3.1
8	1	1.8	2	2.6	-	-
No children and missing values	18	31.6	19	25.0	34	34.7
Totals	57	100.0	76	100.0	98	100.0

Table 10. Number of domestic servants in the primary households in Horsham: 1851, 1861 and 1871 (10% sample)

| | Number of households of each type | | | | | |
| | 1851 | | 1861 | | 1871 | |
Number of domestic servants	Freq	%	Freq	%	Freq	%
1	14	24.6	14	18.4	19	19.4
2	3	5.3	3	3.9	4	4.1
3	1	1.8	2	2.6	2	2.0
4	-	-	-	-	1	1.0
5	-	-	-	-	1	1.0
7	1	1.8	-	-	-	-
No domestic servants and missing values	38	66.7	57	75.0	71	72.4
Totals	57	100.0	76	100.0	98	100.0

Table 11. Number of lodgers in the primary households in Horsham: 1851, 1861 and 1871 (10% sample)

Number of lodgers

	1851		1861		1871	
1	6	10.5	10	13.2	10	10.2
2	-	-	2	2.6	5	5.1
3	2	3.5	5	6.6	5	5.1
4	1	1.8	-	-	2	2.0
5	-	-	-	-	1	1.0
7	1	1.8	-	-	-	-
No lodgers and missing values	47	82.5	59	77.6	75	76.5
Totals	57	100.0	76	100.0	98	100.0

Table 12. Number of persons in all secondary households in each dwelling unit sharing accommodation in Horsham: 1851, 1861 and 1871 (10% sample)

Number of persons in secondary households per dwelling unit

	1851		1861		1871	
1	1	1.8	1	1.3	-	-
2	2	3.5	-	-	2	2.0
3	-	-	1	1.3	1	1.0
5	-	-	1	1.3	-	-
No secondary household and missing values	54	94.7	73	96.1	95	96.9
Totals	57	100.0	76	100.0	98	100.0

Table 13   Size of primary households in Salisbury : 1851, 1861
           and 1871 (10% sample)

Number of persons in family	Number of households of each type					
	1851		1861		1871	
	Freq	%	Freq	%	Freq	%
1	16	7.1	14	6.0	15	6.0
2	46	20.4	29	12.4	36	14.3
3	31	13.7	37	15.8	47	18.7
4	43	19.0	39	16.7	43	17.1
5	29	12.8	42	17.9	26	10.3
6	19	8.4	25	10.7	28	11.1
7	21	9.3	23	9.8	19	7.5
8	8	3.5	14	6.0	14	5.6
9	6	2.7	6	2.6	9	3.6
10	7	3.1	3	1.3	7	2.8
11	-	-	2	0.9	4	1.6
12	-	-	-	-	1	0.4
13	-	-	-	-	1	0.4
16	-	-	-	-	1	0.4
17	-	-	-	-	1	0.4
Total	226	100.0	234	100.0	252	100.0

Table 14   Type of head of primary households in Salisbury: 1851,
           1861 and 1871 (10% sample)

Type of head of household						
Male unmarried, no children	12	5.3	2	0.9	8	3.2
Male married, no children	37	16.4	33	14.1	45	17.9
Male married, children	109	48.2	128	54.7	130	51.6
Female unmarried, no children	9	4.0	8	3.4	12	4.8
Widower, no children	4	1.8	2	0.9	3	1.2
Widower, children	9	4.0	8	3.4	5	2.0
Widow, no children	14	6.2	15	6.4	10	4.0
Widow, children	20	8.8	23	9.8	24	9.5
Child	2	0.9	-	-	3	1.2
Female unmarried, children	3	1.3	4	1.7	4	1.6
Female married, no children	3	1.3	2	0.9	2	0.8
Female married, children	4	1.8	7	3.0	5	2.0
Domestic servant	-	-	1	0.4	1	0.4
Domestic servant	-	-	1	0.4	-	-
Total	226	100.0	234	100.0	252	100.0

Table 15 Age of head of primary households in Salisbury, 1851
         1861 and 1871 (10% sample)

Age of head of household	Number of households of each type					
	1851		1861		1871	
	Freq	%	Freq	%	Freq	%
-9	1	0.4	-	-	-	-
10-14	-	-	-	-	1	0.4
15-19	1	0.4	3	1.3	2	0.8
20-24	11	4.9	6	2.6	10	4.0
25-29	28	12.4	29	12.4	20	7.9
30-34	26	11.5	33	14.1	33	13.1
35-39	21	9.3	23	9.8	24	9.5
40-44	32	14.2	27	11.5	34	13.5
45-49	19	8.4	36	15.4	32	12.7
50-54	20	8.8	20	8.5	29	11.5
55-59	17	7.5	16	6.8	25	9.9
60-64	14	6.2	11	4.7	16	6.3
65-69	13	5.8	11	4.7	9	3.6
70-74	12	5.3	12	5.1	12	4.8
75-79	4	1.8	4	1.7	3	1.2
80-84	4	1.8	2	0.9	1	0.4
85-89	2	0.9	1	0.4	1	0.4
90-94	1	0.4	-	-	-	-
Total	226	100.0	234	100.0	252	100.0

Table 16 Birthplace of head of primary households in Salisbury:
         1851, 1861 and 1871 (10% sample)

Birthplace of head of household	1851 Freq	%	1861 Freq	%	1871 Freq	%
Sussex excl. Horsham	1	0.4	2	0.9	-	-
Swindon	-	-	-	-	1	0.4
Salisbury	100	44.2	81	34.6	99	39.3
Wilts excl. Salisbury & Swindon	66	29.2	74	31.6	66	26.2
Gosport	-	-	-	-	1	0.4
Hants excl. Farnham & Gosport	13	5.8	30	12.8	17	6.7
Kent	-	-	2	0.9	-	-
Surrey	4	1.8	1	0.4	7	2.8
Surrey London	1	0.4	-	-	-	-
Middlesex London	3	1.3	6	2.6	4	1.6
Middlesex	1	0.4	-	-	1	0.4
Dorset	9	4.0	13	5.6	19	7.5
Somerset	11	4.9	6	2.6	11	4.4
Devonshire	1	0.4	-	-	3	1.2
Gloucestershire	2	0.9	3	1.3	2	0.8
Berkshire	2	0.9	2	0.9	1	0.4
Oxfordshire	-	-	1	0.4	-	-
Buckinghamshire	-	-	1	0.4	-	-
Hertfordshire	-	-	-	-	1	0.4
Suffolk	1	0.4	-	-	1	0.4
Norfolk	-	-	-	-	1	0.4
Cambridgeshire	-	-	-	-	1	0.4

Table 16 (Continued)

Birthplace of head of household	Number of households of each type					
	1851		1861		1871	
	Freq	%	Freq	%	Freq	%
Huntingdonshire	1	0.4	-	-	-	-
Northamptonshire	-	-	-	-	2	0.8
Warwickshire	-	-	1	0.4	-	-
Worcestershire	-	-	1	0.4	-	-
Herefordshire	1	0.4	-	-	-	-
Shropshire	1	0.4	-	-	-	-
Leicestershire	1	0.4	-	-	1	0.4
Lincolnshire	-	-	-	-	1	0.4
Nottinghamshire	-	-	2	0.9	-	-
Lancashire	-	-	-	-	1	0.4
Yorkshire	-	-	1	0.4	1	0.4
Westmoreland	-	-	-	-	1	0.4
Durham	-	-	1	0.4	-	-
Channel Islands	-	-	-	-	1	0.4
Isle of Man	1	0.4	-	-	-	-
Wales	1	0.4	-	-	2	0.8
Ireland	1	0.4	2	0.9	1	0.4
Scotland	1	0.4	1	0.4	2	0.8
France	-	-	-	-	1	0.4
Holland	-	-	-	-	1	0.4
Germany	1	0.4	-	-	-	-
Missing values	2	0.9	3	1.3	1	0.4
Total	226	100.0	234	100.0	252	100.0

Table 17   Social Class of head of primary households in
Salisbury: 1851, 1861 and 1871 (10% sample)

Social class						
1	22	9.7	14	6.0	4	1.6
2	9	4.0	9	3.8	45	17.9
3	110	48.7	130	55.6	118	46.8
4	46	20.4	51	21.8	58	23.0
5	27	11.9	17	7.3	17	6.7
Missing values	12	5.3	13	5.6	10	4.0
Total	226	100.0	234	100.0	252	100.0

Table 18   Industrial group of head of primary households in
Salisbury: 1851, 1861 and 1871 (10% sample)

Industrial group						
Agriculture and Breeding						
Farming	6	2.7	7	3.0	9	3.6
Breeding	1	0.4	-	-	2	0.8
Mining						
Brickmaking	-	-	1	0.4	-	-
Salt and Waterworks	1	0.4	-	-	-	-
Building						
Operative	21	9.3	24	10.3	22	8.7

36

Table 18 (Continued)

Industrial group	1851 Freq	1851 %	1861 Freq	1861 %	1871 Freq	1871 %
Manufacture						
Machinery	–	–	1	0.4	–	–
Tools etc	–	–	–	–	2	0.8
Iron and Steel	1	0.4	3	1.3	2	0.8
Copper, Tin, Lead	3	1.3	–	–	–	–
Gold and Silver	–	–	–	–	3	1.2
Coal and Gas	1	0.4	1	0.4	1	0.4
Chemicals	1	0.4	–	–	–	–
Furs and Leather	1	0.4	–	–	3	1.2
Glue Tallow	1	0.4	3	1.3	1	0.4
Hair etc	2	0.9	2	0.9	–	–
Woodworkers	–	–	1	0.4	5	2.0
Furniture	3	1.3	7	3.0	6	2.4
Carriages and harness	4	1.8	5	2.1	5	2.0
Railway carriages etc	–	–	1	0.4	–	–
Cotton and Silk	3	1.3	–	–	1	0.4
Flax, hemp etc	4	1.8	3	1.3	2	0.8
Dyeing	1	0.4	–	–	–	–
Dress	30	13.3	38	16.2	38	15.1
Sundries	–	–	–	–	1	0.4
Food preparation	2	0.9	–	–	–	–
Baking	8	3.5	6	2.6	6	2.4
Drink preparation	3	1.3	2	0.9	3	1.2
Smoking	3	1.3	1	0.4	–	–
Watches, instruments etc	1	0.4	–	–	3	1.2
Printing	1	0.4	4	1.7	2	0.8
Transport						
Warehouses and docks	1	0.4	2	0.9	1	0.4
Ocean nagivation	1	0.4	–	–	–	–
Railways	2	0.9	6	2.6	6	2.4
Roads	6	2.7	9	3.8	5	2.0
Dealing						
Coals	1	0.4	1	0.4	5	2.0
Raw materials	–	–	2	0.9	2	0.8
Dress	2	0.9	5	2.1	4	1.6
Food	11	4.9	8	3.4	12	4.8
Wines, spirits, hotels	6	2.7	7	3.0	10	4.0
Lodging and coffee houses	1	0.4	1	0.4	–	–
Furniture	–	–	–	–	1	0.4
Stationery and publications	–	–	1	0.4	–	–
Household utensils, ornaments	4	1.8	–	–	2	0.8
General dealers	–	–	–	–	4	1.6
Unspecified	3	1.3	2	0.9	1	0.4
Industrial Service						
Banking, insurance, accounting	3	1.3	–	–	2	0.8
Labour	12	5.3	8	3.4	10	4.0
Public Service and Professional						
Central administration	–	–	2	0.9	2	0.8
Local administration	–	–	–	–	1	0.4
Sanitary administration	–	–	–	–	1	0.4
Army	2	0.9	–	–	2	0.8
Navy	–	–	1	0.4	1	0.4
Police and prisons	1	0.4	2	0.9	–	–
Law	4	1.8	4	1.7	–	–

Table 18 (Continued)

| | Number of households of each type | | | | | |
| | 1851 | | 1861 | | 1871 | |
Industrial Group	Freq	%	Freq	%	Freq	%
Medicine	3	1.3	-	-	2	0.8
. Art and amusement (painting)	1	0.4	-	-	1	0.4
Literature	-	-	1	0.4	-	-
Education	1	0.4	3	1.3	3	1.2
Religion	1	0.4	3	1.3	3	1.2
Domestic and Service						
Indoor	3	1.3	8	3.4	11	4.4
Outdoor.	8	3.5	9	3.8	6	2.4
Extra service	6	2.7	10	4.3	14	5.6
Property owning and Independent	15	6.6	7	3.0	10	4.0
Scholar	1	0.4	-	-	1	0.4
Missing values	25	11.1	22	9.4	12	4.8
Total	226	100.0	234	100.0	252	100.0

Table 19 Age of wife of head of primary households in Horsham:
1851, 1861 and 1871 (10% sample)

Age of wife						
15-19	1	0.4	2	0.9	1	0.4
20-24	13	5.8	7	3.0	10	4.0
25-29	18	8.0	32	13.7	21	8.3
30-34	18	8.0	30	12.8	23	9.1
35-39	21	9.3	22	9.4	23	9.1
40-44	17	7.5	22	9.4	24	9.5
45-49	20	8.8	16	6.8	17	6.7
50-54	12	5.3	6	2.6	21	8.3
55-59	5	2.2	9	3.8	12	4.8
60-64	12	5.3	6	2.6	10	4.0
65-69	3	1.3	3	1.3	5	2.0
70-74	1	0.4	1	0.4	2	0.8
Missing values and no wife	85	37.6	78	33.3	83	32.9
Total	226	100.0	234	100.0	252	100.0

Table 20 Birthplace of wife of head of primary households
in Salisbury: 1851, 1861 and 1871 (10% sample)

Birthplace of wife						
Salisbury	48	21.2	56	23.9	60	23.8
Wilts excl. Salisbury & Swindon	44	19.5	61	26.1	43	17.1
Fareham	-	-	-	-	1	0.4
Hants excl. Fareham & Gosport	16	7.1	12	5.1	16	6.3
Kent	-	-	-	-	1	0.4
Surrey	3	1.3	3	1.3	2	0.8
Middlesex London	4	1.8	3	1.3	1	0.4
Dorset	9	4.0	5	2.1	15	6.0
Somerset	8	3.5	4	1.7	9	3.6
Devonshire	1	0.4	2	0.9	2	0.8
Gloucestershire	-	-	-	-	3	1.2
Berkshire	3	1.3	-	-	-	-
Oxfordshire	-	-	1	0.4	1	0.4

Table 20 (Continued)

| | Number of households of each type | | | | | |
| | 1851 | | 1861 | | 1871 | |
Birthplace of wife	Freq	%	Freq	%	Freq	%
Bedfordshire	-	-	2	0.9	-	-
Hertfordshire	-	-	1	0.4	-	-
Suffolk	-	-	-	-	2	0.8
Norfolk	1	0.4	-	-	1	0.4
Cambridgeshire	-	-	-	-	1	0.4
Warwickshire	1	0.4	-	-	1	0.4
Shropshire	-	-	1	0.4	-	-
Staffordshire	-	-	-	-	2	0.8
Nottinghamshire	-	-	1	0.4	1	0.4
Lancashire	1	0.4	-	-	-	-
Yorkshire	1	0.4	1	0.4	1	0.4
Wales	-	-	1	0.4	1	0.4
Ireland	-	-	-	-	2	0.8
Scotland	-	-	-	-	1	0.4
Persia	-	-	1	0.4	-	-
East Indies	-	-	1	0.4	-	-
Missing values and no wife	86	38.1	78	33.3	85	33.7
Total	226	100.0	234	100.0	252	100.0

Table 21 Industrial group of wife of head of primary households in Salisbury: 1851, 1861 and 1871 (10% sample)

Industrial group	Freq	%	Freq	%	Freq	%
Agriculture and Breeding						
Farming	-	-	-	-	1	0.4
Manufacture						
Hair etc	1	0.4	-	-	-	-
Furniture	-	-	-	-	1	0.4
Cotton and Silk	1	0.4	-	-	-	-
Dress	9	4.0	11	4.7	14	5.6
Smoking	1	0.4	-	-	-	-
Dealing						
Food	-	-	1	0.4	-	-
Wines, spirits, hotels	2	0.9	-	-	1	0.4
Lodging and Coffee houses	2	0.9	-	-	-	-
Unspecified	-	-	1	0.4	-	-
Public Service and Professional						
Education	1	0.4	1	0.4	-	-
Domestic Service						
Indoor	1	0.4	2	0.9	3	1.2
Outdoor	7	3.1	6	2.6	6	2.4
Missing values and no wife	201	88.9	212	90.6	226	89.7
Total	226	100.0	234	100.0	252	100.0

Table 22   Number of children of the head and/or wife in the
primary households in Salisbury: 1851, 1861 and 1871
(10% sample)

Number of children	1851 Freq	1851 %	1861 Freq	1861 %	1871 Freq	1871 %
	Number of households of each type					
1	45	19.9	46	19.7	56	22.2
2	38	16.8	39	16.7	33	13.1
3	30	13.3	35	15.0	25	9.9
4	10	4.4	23	9.8	18	7.1
5	14	6.2	17	7.3	21	8.3
6	4	1.8	6	2.6	12	4.8
7	4	1.8	3	1.3	3	1.2
8	1	0.4	1	0.4	4	1.6
No children and missing values	80	35.4	64	27.4	80	31.7
Total	226	100.0	234	100.0	252	100.0

Table 23 Number of domestic servants in the primary households
in Salisbury: 1851, 1861 and 1871 (10% sample)

Number of domestic servants

	Freq	%	Freq	%	Freq	%
1	34	15.0	30	12.8	32	12.7
2	9	4.0	8	3.4	6	2.4
3	2	0.9	4	1.7	2	0.8
4	1	0.4	1	0.4	-	-
5	-	-	1	0.4	-	-
6	-	-	-	-	1	0.4
No domestic servant and missing values	180	79.6	190	81.2	211	83.7
Total	226	100.0	234	100.0	252	100.0

Table 24   Number of lodgers in the primary households in Salisbury: 1851, 1861 and 1871 (10% sample)

| | Number of households of each type | | | | | |
| | 1851, | | 1861 | | 1871 | |
Number of lodgers	Freq	%	Freq	%	Freq	%
1	32	14.2	35	15.0	44	17.5
2	10	4.4	19	8.1	18	7.1
3	1	0.4	9	3.8	7	2.8
4	3	1.3	-	-	2	0.8
5	-	-	-	-	3	1.2
6	1	0.4	-	-	-	-
7	1	0.4	-	-	-	-
9	-	-	-	-	1	0.4
12	-	-	-	-	1	0.4
No lodgers and missing values	178	78.8	171	73.1	176	69.8
Total	226	100.0	234	100.0	252	100.0

Table 25   Number of persons in all secondary households in each dwelling unit sharing accommodation in Salisbury: 1851,1861 and 1971 (10% sample)

Number of persons in secondary households per dwelling unit						
1	1	0.4	1	0.4	6	2.4
2	13	5.8	8	3.4	6	2.4
3	1	0.4	2	0.9	4	1.6
4	5	2.2	3	1.3	-	-
5	2	0.9	2	0.9	-	-
6	-	-	-	-	1	0.4
7	-	-	1	0.4	1	0.4
8	-	-	1	0.4	-	-
10	-	-	1	0.4	-	-
12	-	-	-	-	1	0.4
No secondary household and missing values	204	90.3	215	91.9	233	92.5
Total	226	100.0	234	100.0	252	100.0

Table 26 Size of secondary households in Salisbury: 1851, 1861 and 1871 (10% sample)

Number of persons in family	Number of households of each type					
	1851		1861		1871	
	Freq	%	Freq	%	Freq	%
1	2	8.3	3	12.5	3	16.7
2	16	66.7	11	45.8	7	38.9
3	3	12.5	2	8.3	4	22.2
4	2	8.3	4	16.7	1	5.6
5	1	4.2	2	8.3	1	5.6
6	-	-	-	-	2	11.1
7	-	-	1	4.2	-	-
8	-	-	1	4.2	-	-
Total	24	100.0	24	100.0	18	100.0

Table 27 Type of head of secondary households in Salisbury: 1851, 1861 and 1871 (10% sample)

Type of head of household						
Male unmarried, no children	1	4.2	2	8.3	-	-
Male married, no children	8	33.3	10	41.7	4	22.2
Male married, children	5	20.8	8	33.3	7	38.9
Female unmarried, no children	2	8.3	-	-	-	-
Widower, children	1	4.2	-	-	-	-
Widow, no children	2	8.3	1	4.2	3	16.7
Widow, children	3	12.5	1	4.2	3	16.7
Female unmarried, children	2	8.3	1	4.2	-	-
Female married, children	-	-	1	4.2	1	5.6
Total	24	100.0	24	100.0	18	100.0

Table 28 Age of head of secondary households in Salisbury: 1851, 1861 and 1871 (10% sample)

Age of head of household						
15-19	1	4.2	-	-	-	-
20-24	2	8.3	5	20.8	4	22.2
25-29	5	20.8	4	16.7	2	11.1
30-34	1	4.2	3	12.5	2	11.1
35-39	2	8.3	1	4.2	-	-
40-44	4	16.7	4	16.7	1	5.6
45-49	2	8.3	-	-	1	5.6
50-54	-	-	-	-	1	5.6
55-59	3	12.5	3	12.5	1	5.6
60-64	1	4.2	1	4.2	1	5.6
65-69	2	8.3	-	-	-	-
70-74	1	4.2	2	8.3	1	5.6
75-79	-	-	-	-	3	16.7
80-84	-	-	1	4.2	1	5.6
Total	24	100.0	24	100.0	18	100.0

Table 29 Birthplace of head of secondary households in Salisbury:
1851, 1861 and 1871 (10% sample)

Birthplace of head of household	Number of households of each type					
	1851		1861		1871	
	Freq	%	Freq	%	Freq	%
Salisbury	8	33.3	9	37.5	3	16.7
Wilts excl Salisbury & Swindon	9	37.5	8	33.3	6	33.3
Hants excl. Fareham & Gosport	3	12.5	3	12.5	2	11.1
Dorset	1	4.2	2	8.3	2	11.1
Somserset	1	4.2	-	-	-	-
Devonshire	1	4.2	-	-	-	-
Berkshire	1	4.2	-	-	-	-
Buckinghamshire	-	-	1	4.2	-	-
Warwickshire	-	-	1	4.2	-	-
Lincolnshire	-	-	-	-	1	5.6
Lancashire	-	-	-	-	1	5.6
Wales	-	-	-	-	1	5.6
France	-	-	-	-	1	5.6
Missing values	-	-	-	-	1	5.6
Total	24	100.0	24	100.0	18	100.0

Table 30 Social class of head of secondary households in
Salisbury in 1851, 1861, 1871 (10% sample)

Social class						
1	2	8.3	-	-	1	5.6
2	-	-	-	-	1	5.6
3	11	45.8	15	62.5	9	50.0
4	9	37.5	.3	12.5	3	16.7
5	1	4.2	5	20.8	1	5.6
Missing values	1	4.2	1	4.2	3	16.7
Total	24	100.0	24	100.0	18	100.0

Table 31 Industrial group of head of secondary households in
Salsibury: 1851, 1861 and 1871 (10% sample)

Industrial group	1851 Freq	%	1861 Freq	%	1871 Freq	%
Agriculture and breeding						
Farming	1	4.2	1	4.2	–	–
Fishing	–	–	1	4.2	–	–
Building						
Operative	–	–	6	25.0	1	5.6
Manufacture						
Woodworkers	2	8.3	–	–	–	–
Furniture	–	–	1	4.2	1	5.6
Carriages and harness	–	–	–	–	1	5.6
Flax, hemp etc	1	4.2	–	–	–	–
Dress	5	20.8	2	8.3	3	16.7
Baking	1	4.2	–	–	–	–
Printing	–	–	–	–	1	5.6
Transport						
Warehouses and docks	–	–	1	4.2	–	–
Railways	–	–	1	4.2	1	5.6
Roads	3	12.5	1	4.2	–	–
Dealing						
Raw materials	1	4.2	–	–	–	–
Dress	–	–	1	4.2	1	5.6
Food	–	–	1	4.2	–	–
Wines, spirits, hotels	–	–	1	4.2	–	–
Industrial Service						
Labour	–	–	3	12.5	–	–
Public Service and Professional						
Central administration	1	4.2	–	–	1	5.6
Law	1	4.2	–	–	–	–
Medicine	–	–	1	4.2	–	–
Domestic Service						
Indoor	2	8.3	–	–	2	11.1
Outdoor	1	4.2	–	–	1	5.6
Extra service	2	8.3	1	4.2	–	–
Property Owning and Independent	1	4.2	–	–	1	5.6
Missing values	2	8.3	2	8.3	4	22.2
Total	24	100.0	24	100.0	18	100.0

Table 32 Age of wife of head of secondary households in Salisbury:
1851, 1861 and 1871 (10% sample)

Age of wife	1851	%	1861	%	1871	%
15–19	–	–	2	8.3	–	–
20–24	3	12.5	2	8.3	4	22.2
25–29	3	12.5	3	12.5	3	16.7
30–34	1	4.2	2	8.3	–	–
35–39	2	8.3	1	4.2	–	–
40–44	–	–	1	4.2	1	5.6
45–49	2	8.3	1	4.2	–	–
50–54	1	4.2	1	4.2	–	–
55–59	–	–	2	8.3	–	–
60–64	–	–	2	8.3	–	–
70–74	–	–	–	–	2	11.1
Missing values and no wives present	12	50.0	7	29.2	8	44.4
Totals	24	100.0	24	100.0	18	1.00

Table 33 Birthplace of wife of head of secondary households
in Salisbury: 1851, 1861, 1871 (10% sample)

| Birthplace of wife | Number of households of each type | | | | | |
| | 1851 | | 1861 | | 1871 | |
	Freq	%	Freq	%	Freq	%
Salisbury	3	12.5	3	12.5	1	5.6
Wilts excl Salisbury & Swindon	6	25.0	8	33.3	2	11.1
Hants excl Fareham & Gosport	1	4.2	2	8.3	1	5.6
Surrey	-	-	-	-	1	5.6
Dorset	2	8.3	1	4.2	1	5.6
Somerset	=	-	-	-	2	11.1
Buckinghamshire	-	-	1	4.2	-	-
Nottinghamshire	-	-	-	-	1	5.6
Yorkshire	-	-	1	4.2	-	-
Ireland	-	-	1	4.2	-	-
France	-	-	-	-	1	5.6
Missing values and no wife	12	50.0	7	29.2	8	44.4
Total	24	100.0	24	100.0	18	100.0

Table 34 Number of children of the head and/or wife in the
secondary households in Salisbury: 1851, 1861 and 1871
(10% sample)

Number of children						
1	7	29.2	7	29.2	6	33.3
2	3	12.5	1	4.2	2	11.1
3	1	4.2	2	8.3	2	11.1
4	-	-	-	-	1	5.6
6	-	-	1	4.2	-	-
No children and missing values	13	54.2	13	54.2	7	38.9
Total	24	100.0	24	100.0	18	100.0

Table 35 Size of primary households in Swindon: 1851, 1861 and 1871 (10% sample)

Number of persons in family	1851 Freq	1851 %	1861 Freq	1861 %	1871 Freq	1871 %
1	1	1.2	2	1.7	2	1.1
2	7	8.2	22	18.2	25	13.4
3	10	11.8	25	20.7	21	11.3
4	16	18.8	17	14.0	36	19.4
5	14	16.5	10	8.3	23	12.4
6	10	11.8	15	12.4	21	11.3
7	12	14.1	10	8.3	20	10.8
8	7	8.2	11	9.1	15	8.1
9	3	3.5	4	3.3	11	5.9
10	2	2.4	2	1.7	4	2.2
11	2	2.4	1	0.8	6	3.2
12	-	-	2	1.7	-	-
13	-	-	-	-	1	0.5
14	1	1.2	-	-	-	-
15	-	-	-	-	1	0.5
Total	85	100.0	121	100.0	186	100.0

Table 36 Type of head of primary households in Swindon: 1851, 1861 and 1871 (10% sample)

Type of head of household						
Male unmarried, no children	1	1.2	2	1.7	1	0.5
Male married, no children	13	15.3	25	20.7	30	16.1
Male married, children	63	74.1	81	66.9	124	66.7
Female unmarried, no children	-	-	2	1.7	-	-
Widower, no children	-	-	-	-	1	0.5
Widower, children	3	3.5	7	5.8	8	4.3
Widow, no children	1	1.2	1	0.8	6	3.2
Widow, children	4	4.7	1	0.8	13	7.0
Female married, children	-	-	1	0.8	2	1.1
Lodger	-	-	1	0.8	1	0.5
Total	85	100.0	121	100.0	186	100.0

Table 37 Age of head of primary households in Swindon: 1851,
         1861 and 1871 (10% sample)

| Age of head of household | Number of households of each type | | | | | |
| | 1851 | | 1861 | | 1871 | |
	Freq	%	Freq	%	Freq	%
15-19	1	1.2	-	-	1	0.5
20-24	5	5.9	6	5.0	6	3.2
25-29	11	12.9	22	18.2	24	12.9
30-34	18	21.2	15	12.4	34	18.3
35-39	12	14.1	9	7.4	19	10.2
40-44	15	17.6	20	16.5	19	10.2
45-49	6	7.1	21	17.4	23	12.4
50-54	12	14.1	11	9.1	24	12.9
55-59	1	1.2	6	5.0	11	5.9
60-64	1	1.2	5	4.1	12	6.5
65-69	1	1.2	4	3.3	4	2.2
70-74	-	-	-	-	6	3.2
75-79	1	1.2	-	-	2	1.1
80-84	-	-	-	-	-	-
85-89	-	-	-	-	-	-
90-94	1	1.2	-	-	1	0.5
Missing values	-	-	2	1.7	-	-
Total	85	100.0	121	100.0	186	100.0

Table 38 Birthplace of head of primary households in Swindon:
         1851, 1861 and 1871 (10% sample)

Birthplace of head of household						
Swindon	18	21.2	25	20.7	25	13.4
Wilts excl Salisbury & Swindon	18	21.2	33	27.3	54	29.0
Hampshire	1	1.2	2	1.7	3	1.6
Kent	-	-	1	0.8	3	1.6
Surrey	1	1.2	1	0.8	-	-
Surrey London	-	-	-	-	4	2.2
Middlesex London	2	2.4	2	1.7	8	4.3
Middlesex	-	-	3	2.5	-	-
Dorset	1	1.2	2	1.7	5	2.7
Somerset	4	4.7	7	5.8	14	7.5
Devonshire	3	3.5	2	1.7	4	2.2
Cornwall	-	-	1	0.8	-	-
Gloucestershire	8	9.4	15	12.4	18	9.7
Berkshire	6	7.1	3	2.5	8	4.3
Oxfordshire	2	2.4	3	2.5	4	2.2
Buckinghamshire	1	1.2	1	0.8	1	0.5
Bedfordshire	-	-	-	-	1	0.5
Hertfordshire	-	-	1	0.8	1	0.5
Norfolk	-	-	-	-	1	0.5
Warwickshire	2	2.4	-	-	1	0.5
Worcestershire	-	-	-	-	1	0.5
Shropshire	-	-	-	-	1	0.5
Staffordshire	2	2.4	-	-	1	0.5

Table 38 (Continued)

Birthplace of head of household	1851 Freq	%	1861 Freq	%	1871 Freq	%
		Number of households of each type				
Derbyshire	–	–	1	0.8	–	–
Cheshire	–	–	–	–	1	0.5
Lancashire	1	1.2	3	2.5	4	2.2
Yorkshire	2	2.4	3	2.5	2	1.1
Westmoreland	–	–	2	1.7	–	–
Cumberland	1	1.2	1	0.8	–	–
Durham 2	2	2.4	1	0.8	1	0.5
Northumberland	3	3.5	–	–	3	1.6
Isle of Man	–	–	–	–	1	0.5
Wales	–	–	–	–	11	5.9
Ireland	1	1.2	1	0.8	1	0.5
Scotland	4	4.7	7	5.8	4	2.2
Missing values	2	2.4	–	–	–	–
Total	85	100.0	121	100.0	186	100.0

Table 39 Social class of head of primary households in Swindon: 1851, 1861 and 1871 (10% sample)

Social class						
1	5	5.9	3	2.5	6	3.2
2	3	3.5	6	5.0	10	5.4
3	48	56.5	75	62.0	120	64.5
4	20	23.5	29	24.0	28	15.1
5	8	9.4	6	5.0	14	7.5
Missing values	1	1.2	2	1.7	8	4.3
Total	85	100.0	121	100.0	186	100.0

Table 40 Industrial group of head of primary households in Swindon: 1851, 1861 and 1871 (10% sample)

Industrial group						
Agriculture and Breeding						
Farming	13	15.3	10	8.3	5	2.7
Mining						
Quarrying	–	–	1	0.8	1	0.5
Brickmaking	–	–	–	–	2	1.1
Building						
Management	1	1.2	–	–	–	–
Operative	9	10.6	10	8.3	13	7.0
Railway	1	1.2	2	1.7	–	–
Manufacture						
Machinery	5	5.9	8	6.6	9	4.8
Tools	–	–	1	0.8	–	–
Iron and Steel	5	5.9	11	9.1	25	13.4
Copper, Tin, Lead	2	2.4	2	1.7	5	2.7
Coals and gas	1	1.2	3	2.5	–	–
Furs and leather	1	1.2	–	–	–	–
Woodworkers	1	1.2	1	0.8	–	

Table 40 (Continued)

	Number of households of each type					
	1851		1861		1871	
Industrial Group	Freq	%	Freq	%	Freq	%
Furniture	–	–	1	0.8	–	–
Carriages and harness	–	–	2	1.7	4	2.2
Railway carriage	–	–	8	6.6	3	1.6
Flax, hemp etc	1	1.2	–	–	–	–
Dress	7	8.2	6	5.0	8	4.3
Baking	1	1.2	2	1.7	1	0.5
Watches, instruments etc	1	1.2	–	–	1	0.5
Printing	–	–	–	–	1	0.5
Unspecified	7	8.2	9	7.4	32	17.2
Transport						
Inland navigation	–	–	1	0.8	1	0.5
Railways	8	9.4	9	7.4	15	8.1
Dealing						
Coals	–	–	1	0.8	1	0.5
Dress	–	–	4	3.3	2	1.1
Food	3	3.5	7	5.8	7	3.8
Wines, spirits, hotels	2	2.4	3	2.5	7	3.8
Lodging and coffee houses	–	–	–	–	2	1.1
Stationery and publications	–	–	–	–	1	0.5
Household utensils, ornaments	–	–	1	0.8	–	–
General dealers	–	–	1	0.8	1	0.5
Unspecified	1	1.2	–	–	–	–
Industrial Service						
Banking, insurance, etc	1	1.2	–	–	–	–
Labour	5	5.9	7	5.8	11	5.9
Public Service and Professional						
Central administration	1	1.2	1	0.8	1	0.5
Police and Prisons	–	–	1	0.8	–	–
Law	2	2.4	–	–	2	1.1
Médicine	–	–	–	–	1	0.5
Religion	–	–	1	0.8	1	0.5
Domestic Service						
Indoor	–	–	–	–	4	2.2
Outdoor	1	1.2	2	1.7	3	1.6
Extra service	1	1.2	–	–	4	2.2
Property Owning and Independent	1	1.2	3	2.5	4	2.2
Missing values	3	3.5	2	1.7	8	4.3
Totals	85	100.0	121	100.0	186	100.0

Table 41   Age of wife of head of primary households in Swindon:
1851, 1861 and 1871 (10% sample)

Age of wife	1851 Freq	1851 %	1861 Freq	1861 %	1871 Freq	1871 %
15-19	-	-	-	-	3	1.6
20-24	9	10.6	12	9.9	13	7.0
25-29	15	17.6	17	14.0	25	13.4
30-34	12	14.1	14	11.6	17	9.1
35-39	13	15.3	18	14.9	31	16.7
40-44	9	10.6	14	11.6	13	7.0
45-49	6	7.1	11	9.1	16	8.6
50-54	9	10.6	4	3.3	14	7.5
55-59	-	-	11	9.1	7	3.8
60-64	-	-	4	3.3	6	3.2
65-69	-	-	1	0.8	3	1.6
70-74	1	1.2	-	-	1	0.5
75-79	-	-	-	-	-	-
80-84	-	-	-	-	-	-
85-89	-	-	-	-	-	-
90-94	-	-	-	-	-	-
No wives and missing values	11	12.9	15	12.4	37	19.9
Total	85	100.0	121	100.0	186	100.0

Table 42   Birthplace of wife of head of primary households
in Swindon: 1851, 1861 and 1871 (10% sample)

Birthplace of wife	1851 Freq	1851 %	1861 Freq	1861 %	1871 Freq	1871 %
Sussex, exlc Horsham	-	-	-	-	1	0.5
Swindon	10	11.8	15	12.4	20	10.8
Wilts excl Salisbury & Swindon	23	27.1	39	32.2	44	23.7
Hampshire	-	-	2	1.7	2	1.1
Kent	-	-	-	-	2	1.1
Surrey	-	-	-	-	2	1.1
Surrey London	-	-	-	-	2	1.1
Middlesex London	-	-	4	3.3	2	1.1
Middlesex	-	-	2	1.7	2	1.1
Dorset	1	1.2	-	-	-	-
Somerset	11	12.9	8	6.6	14	7.5
Devonshire	2	2.4	1	0.8	4	2.2
Cornwall	-	-	3	2.5	-	-
Gloucestershire	4	4.7	9	7.4	13	7.0
Berkshire	6	7.1	6	5.0	7	3.8
Oxfordshire	-	-	1	0.8	3	1.6
Buckinghamshire	1	1.2	2	1.7	1	0.5
Hertfordshire	-	-	-	-	1	0.5
Warwickshire	1	1.2	-	-	2	1.1
Herefordshire	-	-	1	0.8	1	0.5
Shropshire	-	-	-	-	1	0.5
Rutland	-	-	-	-	1	0.5
Lincolnshire	1	1.2	-	-	-	-

Table 42 (Continued)

| | Number of households in each type | | | | | |
| Birthplace of wife | 1851 | | 1861 | | 1871 | |
	Freq	%	Freq	%	Freq	%
Derbyshire	-	-	1	0.8	1	0.5
Cheshire	-	-	-	-	1	0.5
Lancashire	3	3.5	-	-	1	0.5
Yorkshire	2	2.4	3	2.5	1	0.5
Westmoreland	-	-	2	1.7	1	0.5
Cumberland	-	-	1	0.8	1	0.5
Durham	2	2.4	1	0.8	-	-
Northumberland	2	2.4	-	-	-	-
Wales	1	1.2	-	-	8	4.2
Ireland	1	1.2	1	0.8	1	0.5
Scotland	3	3.5	2	1.7	6	3.2
France	-	-	-	-	1	0.5
Africa	-	-	1	0.8	1	0.5
No wife and missing values	11	12.9	16	13.2	38	20.4
Total	85	100.0	121	100.0	186	100.0

Table 43   Industrial group of wife of head of primary households in Swindon: 1851, 1861 and 1871 (10% sample)

Industrial group of wife						
Agriculture and Breeding						
Farming	-	-	3	2.5	-	-
Manufacture						
Dress	4	4.7	2	1.7	2	1.1
Dealing						
Wines, spirits, hotels	-	-	-	-	1	0.5
Public Service and Professional						
Education	-	-	-	-	2	1.1
Domestic Service						
Indoor	-	-	1	0.8	1	0.5
Extra service	2	2.4	4	3.3	1	0.5
Unoccupied	79	92.9	111	91.7	179	96.2
Total	85	100.0	121	100.0	186	100.0

Table 44   Number of children of the head and/or wife in the
           primary households in Swindon: 1851, 1861 and 1871
           (10% sample)

| | Number of households of each type | | | | | |
| | 1851 | | 1861 | | 1871 | |
Number of children	Freq	%	Freq	%	Freq	%
1	15	17.6	30	24.8	45	24.2
2	16	18.8	13	10.7	31	16.7
3	12	14.1	13	10.7	19	10.2
4	9	10.6	14	11.6	19	10.2
5	8	9.4	6	5.0	12	6.5
6	6	7.1	9	7.4	7	3.8
7	2	2.4	4	3.3	8	4.3
8	1	1.2	-	-	2	1.1
9	-	-	1	0.8	2	1.1
10	-	-	-	-	-	-
11	1	1.2	-	-	1	0.5
No children	15	17.6	31	25.6	40	21.5
Total	85	100.0	121	100.0	186	100.0

Table 45   Number of domestic servants in the primary households
           in Swindon: 1851, 1861 and 1871 (10% sample)

Number of domestic servants						
1	9	10.6	11	9.1	23	12.4
2	1	1.2	2	1.7	3	1.6
3	-	-	-	-	1	0.5
4	1	1.2	-	-	-	-
No domestic servants	74	87.1	108	89.3	159	85.5
Total	85	100.0	121	100.0	186	100.0

Table 46   Number of lodgers in the primary households in Swindon:
           1851, 1861 1871 (10% sample)

| | Number of households of each type | | | | | |
| | 1851 | | 1861 | | 1871 | |
Number of lodgers	Freq	%	Freq	%	Freq	%
1	13	15.3	16	13.2	29	15.6
2	4	4.7	4	3.3	19	10.2
3	1	1.2	1	0.8	4	2.2
4	1	1.2	1	0.8	5	2.7
5	-	-	-	-	5	2.7
6	-	-	-	-	-	-
7	-	-	-	-	-	-
8	1	1.2	-	-	-	-
No lodgers	65	76.5	99	81.8	124	66.7
Total	85	100.0	121	100.0	186	100.0

Table 47   Number of persons in all secondary households in each
           dwelling unit sharing accommodation in Swindon:
           1851, 1861 and 1871 (10% sample)

Number of persons in secondary households per dwelling unit						
1	1	1.2	-	-	1	0.5
2	2	2.4	4	3.3	12	6.5
3	2	2.4	4	3.3	8	4.3
4	1	1.2	4	3.3	11	5.9
5	1	1.2	3	2.5	4	2.2
6	-	-	1	0.8	2	1.1
7	1	1.2	-	-	1	0.5
8	2	2.4	1	0.8	1	0.5
9	-	-	-	-	3	1.6
10	-	-	-	-	3	1.6
11	-	-	-	-	-	-
12	-	-	-	-	1	0.5
15	-	-	-	-	2	1.1
No secondary households	75	88.2	104	86.0	137	73.7
Total	85	100.0	121	100.0	186	100.0

Table 48 Size of secondary households in Swindon: 1851, 1861
and 1871 (10% sample)

	Number of households of each type					
Number of persons	1851		1861		1871	
in household	Freq	%	Freq	%	Freq	%
1	1	7.7	1	4.8	-	-
2	4	30.8	7	33.3	22	32.8
3	4	30.8	5	23.8	16	23.9
4	1	7.7	5	23.8	13	19.4
5	2	15.4	3	14.3	7	10.4
6	-	-	-	-	5	7.5
7	-	-	-	-	2	3.0
8	1	7.7	-	-	1	1.5
9	-	-	-	-	-	-
10	-	-	-	-	1	1.5
Total	13	100.0	21	100.0	67	100.0

Table 49 Type of head of secondary households in Swindon: 1851,
1861 and 1871 (10% sample)

Type of head of household						
Male unmarried, no children	1	7.7	-	-	1	1.5
Male married, no children	4	30.8	6	28.6	25	37.3
Male married, children	5	38.5	9	42.9	36	53.7
Widower, no children	-	-	1	4.8	-	-
Widower, children	-	-	2	9.5	1	1.5
Widow, no children	-	-	-	-	1	1.5
Widow, children	3	23.1	2	9.5	3	4.5
Female married, children	-	-	1	4.8	-	-
Total	13	100.0	21	100.0	67	100.0

Table 50 Age of head of secondary households in Swindon: 1851,
1861 and 1871 (10% sample)

| | Number of households of each type | | | | | |
| | 1851 | | 1861 | | 1871 | |
Age of head of household	Freq	%	Freq	%	Freq	%
15-19	1	7.7	-	-	-	-
20-24	1	7.7	1	4.8	10	14.9
25-29	3	23.1	6	28.6	22	32.8
30-34	3	23.1	2	9.5	14	20.9
35-39	1	7.7	1	4.8	7	10.4
40-44	-	-	2	9.5	5	7.5
45-49	1	7.7	4	19.0	2	3.0
50-54	2	15.4	-	-	3	4.5
55-59	-	-	1	4.8	1	1.5
60-64	-	-	2	9.5	2	3.0
65-69	1	7.7	1	4.8	1	1.5
75-79	-	-	1	4.8	-	-
Total	13	100.0	21	100.0	67	100.0

Table 51 Birthplace of head of secondary households in Swindon:
1851, 1861 and 1871 (10% sample)

Birthplace of head of household						
Sussex except Horsham	-	-	3	14.3	1	1.5
Swindon	-	-	-	-	8	11.9
Wilts excl Salisbury & Swindon	4	30.8	6	28.6	14	20.9
Hampshire	-	-	-	-	1	1.5
Kent	-	-	-	-	1	1.5
Surrey	1	7.7	-	-	-	-
Middlesex London	1	7.7	1	4.8	3	4.5
Somerset	1	7.7	3	14.3	7	10.4
Devonshire	-	-	-	-	1	1.5
Gloucestershire	1	7.7	3	14.3	7	10.4
Berkshire	2	15.4	1	4.8	3	4.5
Oxfordshire	-	-	-	-	2	3.0
Buckinghamshire	-	-	-	-	1	1.5
Warwickshire	-	-	-	-	2	3.0
Herefordshire	-	-	-	-	1	1.5
Shropshire	-	-	-	-	1	1.5
Staffordshire	-	-	-	-	2	3.0
Lancashire	-	-	-	-	1	1.5
Yorkshire	-	-	1	4.8	1	1.5
Cumberland	-	-	-	-	1	1.5
Wales	1	7.7	2	9.5	5	7.5
Ireland	1	7.7	-	-	2	3.0
Scotland	-	-	1	4.8	2	3.0
West Indies	1	7.7	-	-	-	-
Total	13	100.0	21	100.0	67	100.0

Table 52 Social class of head of secondary households in
Swindon: 1851, 1861 and 1871 (10% sample)

	Number of households of each type					
	1851		1861		1871	
Social class	Freq	%	Freq	%	Freq	%
1	-	-	1	4.8	-	-
2	1	7.7	-	-	1	1.5
3	7	53.8	10	47.6	44	65.7
4	3	23.1	7	33.3	14	20.9
5	2	15.4	1	4.8	7	10.4
Missing values	-	-	2	9.5	1	1.5
Total	13	100.0	21	100.0	67	100.0

Table 53 Industrial group of head of secondary households in
Swindon: 1851, 1861 and 1871 (10% sample)

Industrial group						
Agriculture and Breeding						
Farming	1	7.7	3	14.3	-	-
Mining						
Quarrying	-	-	-	-	1	1.5
Building						
Operative	2	15.4	-	-	13	19.4
Railway	-	-	1	4.8	-	-
Manufacture						
Machinery	2	15.4	3	14.3	2	3.0
Iron and Steel	-	-	1	4.8	17	25.4
Copper, Tin, Lead	-	-	-	-	1	1.5
Furniture	-	-	1	4.8	2	3.0
Carriages and harness	1	7.7	-	-	1	1.5
Railway carriages	-	-	1	4.8	4	6.0
Paper	-	-	-	-	1	1.5
Dress	1	7.7	2	9.5	1	1.5
Printing	-	-	1	4.8	-	-
Unspecified	1	7.7	1	4.8	7	10.4
Transport						
Railways	1	7.7	1	4.8	1	1.5
Dealing						
Coals	-	-	1	4.8	-	-
Food	-	-	-	-	4	6.0
Industrial Service						
Labour	-	-	1	4.8	7	10.4
Public Service and Professional						
Law	-	-	-	-	1	1.5
Medicine	1	7.7	1	4.8	-	-
Art and Amusement (painting)	-	-	-	-	1	1.5
Art and Amusement (music)	-	-	-	-	1	1.5
Domestic Service						
Indoor	-	-	1	4.8	-	-
Outdoor	1	7.7	-	-	-	-
Property Owning and Independent	-	-	-	-	1	1.5
Missing values	2	15.4	2	9.5	1	1.5
Total	13	100.0	21	100.0	67	100.0

Table 54 Age of wife of head of secondary households in Swindon: 1851, 1861 and 1871 (10% sample)

| | Number of households of each type | | | | | |
| | 1851 | | 1861 | | 1871 | |
Age of wife	Freq	%	Freq	%	Freq	%
15-19	-	-	-	-	1	1.5
20-24	1	7.7	3	14.3	13	19.4
25-29	2	15.4	3	14.3	15	22.4
30-34	2	15.4	3	14.3	19	28.4
35-39	2	15.4	1	4.8	4	6.0
40-44	-	-	2	9.5	2	3.0
45-49	-	-	1	4.8	3	4.5
50-54	-	-	1	4.8	-	-
55-59	-	-	-	-	1	1.5
60-64	-	-	1	4.8	-	-
65-69	1	7.7	-	-	1	1.5
Missing values and household with no wife	5	38.5	6	28.6	8	11.9
Total	13	100.0	21	100.0	67	100.0

Table 55 Birthplace of wife of head of secondary households in Swindon: 1851, 1861 and 1871 (10% sample)

Birthplace of wife	Freq	%	Freq	%	Freq	%
Swindon	1	7.7	2	9.5	3	4.5
Wilts excl Salisbury & Swindon	3	23.1	5	23.8	11	16.4
Hampshire	-	-	-	-	2	3.0
Surrey London	-	-	-	-	2	3.0
Middlesex London	2	15.4	-	-	2	3.0
Middlesex	-	-	-	-	1	1.5
Dorset	-	-	1	4.8	1	1.5
Somerset	1	7.7	1	4.8	5	7.5
Devonshire	-	-	-	-	1	1.5
Gloucestershire	-	-	-	-	4	6.0
Berkshire	1	7.7	1	4.8	2	3.0
Oxfordshire	-	-	-	-	4	6.0
Buckinghamshire	-	-	-	-	1	1.5
Essex	-	-	-	-	1	1.5
Huntingdonshire	-	-	1	4.8	-	-
Warwickshire	-	-	-	-	2	3.0
Worcestershire	-	-	-	-	3	4.5
Staffordshire	-	-	1	4.8	2	3.0
Lincolnshire	-	-	-	-	1	1.5
Lancashire	-	-	-	-	1	1.5
Yorkshire	-	-	1	4.8	-	-
Cumberland	-	-	-	-	1	1.5
Wales	-	-	-	-	4	6.0
Ireland	-	-	1	4.8	1	1.5
Scotland	-	-	1	4.8	3	4.5
Missing values and household with no wife	5	38.5	6	28.6	9	13.4
Total	13	100.0	21	100.0	67	100.0

Table 56 Industrial group of wife of head of secondary households in Swindon: 1851, 1861 and 1871 (10% sample)

	Number of households of each type					
	1851		1861		1871	
Industrial group of wife	Freq	%	Freq	%	Freq	%
Manufacture						
Dress	-	-	-	-	3	4.5
Domestic Service						
Indoor	-	-	1	4.8	1	1.5
Extra service	-	-	-	-	1	1.5
Missing values and no wife	13	100.0	20	95.2	62	92.5
Total	13	100.0	21	100.0	67	100.0

Table 57 Number of children of the head and/or wife in the secondary households in Swindon: 1851, 1861 and 1871 (10% sample)

Number of children						
1	3	23.1	7	33.3	15	22.4
2	2	15.4	4	19.0	14	20.9
3	2	15.4	1	4.8	3	4.5
4	1	7.7	2	9.5	5	7.5
5	-	-	-	-	2	3.0
6	-	-	-	-	1	1.5
No children	5	38.5	7	33.3	27	40.3
Total	13	100.0	21	100.0	67	100.0

Table 58 Number of domestic servants in the secondary households in Swindon: 1851, 1861 and 1871 (10% sample)

Number of domestic servants						
No domestic servants	13	100.0	21	100.0	67	100.0
Total	13	100.0	21	100.0	67	100.0

Table 59 Number of lodgers in the secondary households in Swindon: 1851, 1861 and 1871 (10% sample)

Number of lodgers						
1	-	-	-	-	5	7.5
2	-	-	-	-	4	6.0
3	1	7.7	-	-	1	1.5
8	-	-	-	-	1	1.5
No lodgers	12	92.3	21	100.0	56	83.6
Total	13	100.0	21	100.0	67	100.0

Table 60   Comparison between sizes of primary households
           in New and Old Swindon, 1871 (10% sample)

| Number of persons in family | Number of households of each type | | | |
| | New Swindon | | Old Swindon | |
	Freq	%	Freq	%
1	1	1.2	1	1.0
2	12	14.5	13	12.6
3	12	14.5	9	8.7
4	11	13.3	25	24.3
5	9	10.8	14	13.6
6	11	13.3	10	9.7
7	11	13.3	9	8.7
8	5	6.0	10	9.7
9	8	9.6	3	2.9
10	1	1.2	3	2.9
11	1	1.2	5	4.9
13	1	1.2	-	-
15	-	-	1	1.0
Total	83	100.0	103	100.0

Table 61   Comparison between types of head of primary households
           in New and Old Swindon, 1871 (10% sample)

Type of head of household	New Swindon		Old Swindon	
Male unmarried, no children	-	-	1	1.0
Male married, no children	17	20.5	13	12.6
Male married, children	53	63.9	71	68.9
Widower, no children	-	-	1	1.0
Widower, children	2	2.4	6	5.8
Widow, no children	3	3.6	3	2.9
Widow, children	6	7.2	7	6.8
Female married, children	1	1.2	1	1.0
Lodger	1	1.2	-	-
Total	83	100.0	103	100.0

Table 62 Comparison between age of head of primary households in
New and Old Swindon, 1871 (10% sample)

| Age of head of household | Number of households of each type | | | |
| | New Swindon | | Old Swindon | |
	Freq	%	Freq	%
15-19	-	-	1	1.0
20-24	4	4.8	2	1.9
25-29	13	15.7	11	10.7
30-34	19	22.9	15	14.6
35-39	10	12.0	9	8.7
40-44	9	10.8	10	9.7
45-49	8	9.6	15	14.6
50-54	11	13.3	13	12.6
55-59	5	6.0	6	5.8
60-64	2	2.4	10	9.7
65-69	1	1.2	3	2.9
70-74	1	1.2	5	4.9
75-79	-	-	2	1.9
90-94	-	-	1	1.0
Total	83	100.0	103	100.0

Table 63 Comparison between birthplace of head of households
in New and Old Swindon, 1871 (10% sample)

Birthplace of head of household				
Swindon	5	6.0	20	19.4
Wilts excl Salisbury & Swindon	20	24.1	34	33.0
Hants excl Fareham & Gosport	1	1.2	2	1.9
Kent	1	1.2	2	1.9
Surrey London	2	2.4	2	1.9
Middlesex London	4	4.8	4	3.9
Dorset	2	2.4	3	2.9
Somerset	7	8.4	7	6.8
Devonshire	2	2.4	2	1.9
Gloucestershire	11	13.3	7	6.8
Berkshire	3	3.6	5	4.9
Oxfordshire	2	2.4	2	1.9
Buckinghamshire	1	1.2	-	-
Bedfordshire	-	-	1	1.0
Hertfordshire	1	1.2	-	-
Norfolk	1	1.2	-	-
Warwickshire	-	-	1	1.0
Worcestershire	-	-	1	1.0
Shropshire	-	-	1	1.0
Staffordshire	1	1.2	-	-
Cheshire	1	1.2	-	-
Lancashire	2	2.4	2	1.9
Yorkshire	2	2.4	-	-
Durham	1	1.2	-	-
Northumberland	3	3.6	-	-
Wales	7	8.4	4	3.9
Isle of Man	-	-	1	1.0
Ireland	1	1.2	-	-
Scotland	2	2.4	2	1.9
Total	83	100.0	103	100.0

Table 64 Comparison between social class of head of primary household in New and Old Swindon, 1871 (10% sample)

| | Number of households of each type | | | |
| | New Swindon | | Old Swindon | |
Social class	Freq	%	Freq	%
1	1	1.2	5	4.9
2	2	2.4	8	7.8
3	61	73.5	59	57.3
4	10	12.0	18	17.5
5	3	3.6	11	10.7
Missing values	6	7.2	2	1.9
Total	83	100.2	103	100.0

Table 65 Comparison between industrial group of head of primary households in New and Old Swindon, 1871 (10% sample)

Industrial group	Freq	%	Freq	%
Agriculture and Breeding				
Farming	–	–	5	4.9
Mining				
Quarrying	–	–	1	1.0
Brickmaking	–	–	2	1.9
Building				
Operative	1	1.2	12	11.7
Manufacture				
Machinery	3	3.6	6	5.8
Iron and steel	15	18.1	10	9.7
Copper, tin, lead	3	3.6	2	1.9
Carriages and harness	1	1.2	3	2.9
Railway carriages	1	1.2	2	1.9
Dress	3	3.6	5	4.9
Baking	–	–	1	1.0
Watches, instruments, etc	–	–	1	1.0
Printing	–	–	1	1.0
Unspecified	26	31.3	6	5.8
Transport				
Inland navigation	–	–	1	1.0
Railways	9	10.8	6	5.8
Dealing				
Coals	–	–	1	1.0
Dress	–	–	2	1.9
Food	3	3.6	4	3.9
Wines, spirits, hotels	4	4.8	3	2.9
Lodging and coffeehouses	1	1.2	1	1.0
Stationery and publications	–	–	1	1.0
General dealers	–	–	1	1.0
Industrial Service				
Labour	2	2.4	9	8.7
Public Service and Professional				
Central administration	–	–	1	1.0
Law	–	–	2	1.9
Medicine	–	–	1	1.0
Religion	1	1.2	–	–
Domestic Service				
Indoor	2	2.4	2	1.9
Outdoor	–	–	3	2.9
Extra service	2	2.4	2	1.9
Property Owning and Independent	–	–	4	3.9
Missing values	6	7.2	2	1.9
Total	83	100.0	103	100.0

Table 66   Comparison between number of children of the head and/or wife in the primary households in New and Old Swindon, 1871 (10% sample)

| | Number of households of each type | | | |
| | New Swindon | | Old Swindon | |
Number of children	Freq	%	Freq	%
1	20	24.1	25	24.3
2	8	9.6	23	22.3
3	11	13.3	8	7.8
4	11	13.3	8	7.8
5	6	7.2	6	5.8
6	3	3.6	4	3.9
7	2	2.4	6	5.8
8	–	–	2	1.9
9	–	–	2	1.9
11	1	1.2	–	–
No children and missing values	21	25.3	19	18.4
Total	83	100.0	103	100.0

Table 67   Comparison between number of domestic servants in the primary household in New and Old Swindon, 1871 (10% sample)

Number of domestic servants				
1	7	8.4	16	15.5
2	–	–	3	2.9
3	–	–	1	1.0
No domestic servants	76	91.6	83	80.6
Total	83	100.0	103	100.0

Table 68   Comparison between number of lodgers in the primary households in New and Old Swindon, 1871 (10% sample)

Number of lodgers				
1	18	21.7	11	10.7
2	9	10.8	10	9.7
3	3	3.6	1	1.0
4]	4	4.8	1	1.0
5	2	2.4	3	2.9
No lodgers	47	56.6	77	74.8
Total	83	100.0	103	100.0

Table 69 Number of persons in all secondary households in each
dwelling unit sharing accommodation in New and Old
Swindon, 1871 (10% sample)

Number of persons in secondary households per dwelling unit	Number of households of each type			
	New Swindon		Old Swindon	
	Freq	%	Freq	%
1	1	1.2	–	–
2	4	4.8	8	7.8
3	5	6.0	3	2.9
4	7	8.4	4	3.9
5	3	3.6	1	1.0
6	–	–	2	1.9
7	1	1.2	–	–
8	–	–	1	1.0
9	3	3.6	–	–
10	2	2.4	1	1.0
12	1	1.2	–	–
15	2	2.4	–	–
No secondary households	54	65.1	83	80.6
Total	83	100.0	103	100.0